EQ

emotional intelligence for everyone

Stephanie Vermeulen

EQ

emotional intelligence for everyone

ZEBRA

ZEBRA

Published by Zebra Press
an imprint of Struik Publishers
(a division of New Holland Publishing (South Africa) (Pty) Ltd)
PO Box 1144, Cape Town, 8000
New Holland Publishing is a member of the Johnnic Publishing Group

First published in 1999

5 7 9 10 8 6 4

MANAGING EDITOR Marika Truter
COPY EDITORS Jacqui Greenop
& Tracey Chalmers
COVER DESIGNER Micha McKerr
TEXT DESIGNER Denise Meredith
DTP Denise Meredith

Printed and bound by CTP Book Printers

ISBN 1 86872 331 3

DISCLAIMER
The author and publishers have made every reasonable effort to obtain permission
for the use of the material in appendix 2 — Louis Janda's *The Psychologist's Book
of Self-tests* — but were unsuccessful. The publisher would be pleased to hear
from the copyright holders in question to rectify any errors or omissions.

Contact Stephanie Vermeulen
www.theeqsite.co.za

To Mark
Thanks. You're a star

Acknowledgements

The principles of emotional intelligence make it clear that nobody can succeed on their own; and the writing of this book was no exception. There are many people who have contributed in myriad ways to its creation and I'm inordinately grateful to them all.

In particular, I am grateful to my husband, Mark Porter, who not only read, edited and re-read its many drafts, but also had to put up with the intensity of living with a first-time author. For him, I know it must have been extremely taxing, but throughout his admirable handling of this project, he still managed his special brand of caring and retained a sense of humour.

I owe thanks to Lisa Baggott, an exceptional friend, who waded through the painful process of the first draft and pointed it in the right direction. I am also indebted to my mother, Irene Vermeulen, who is a great writer herself and can spot a dangling participle a few yards away. She tirelessly edited each draft copy while my father, Dirk, made a welcome contribution with his practical suggestions. Additionally, thanks to someone who's been down this road before; John Kehoe very generously mentored my progress – be it in dealing with my author's neurosis or providing much helpful advice and many laughs along the way.

As friends, Norman Roux was instrumental in getting the project started and Gwynne Mathias encouraged and supported me to make it a reality. Thanks are due to my brothers, Keith, Andrew and Ian, for their unwavering belief in me and to my many friends for the welcome and necessary distractions, as well as some important lessons during the process, even the hard ones! This book also could never have happened without the hundreds of authors whose work inspired its creation or without the support of a few courageous clients who, in the early days, went out on a limb to test this new material. Finally, thanks to a very special little girl – Phila Baloyi – who in her innocent way showed me that I'd fallen into the trap of over-editing. She did so by constantly asking: 'Isn't your book finished YET?'

CONTENTS

CONTENTS

Foreword

Since Daniel Goleman launched his book *Emotional Intelligence* in 1995, the global interest in emotional intelligence – EQ – has been tremendous. The concept has created much excitement but unfortunately many authors have only taken an academic or intellectual view.

EQ: Emotional Intelligence for Everyone stands out from the other more complex works because it provides practical steps for understanding the language of one's emotions. It also details how to respond to them so that anyone can learn winning ways.

This book is packed with valuable information that gives practical techniques that everyone can apply to their lives. It's sure to make a profound impact upon whoever reads it. This complex topic is excellently put across in a simple way and so provides the reader with many helpful tools for personal growth.

Stephanie Vermeulen is one of the top visionary thinkers in the country and the best in her field. This publication is an exceptional addition to her work and is sure to stimulate and inspire.

Masterfully written, it's easy to understand and is the best book that I've ever read on EQ.

John Kehoe
June 1999

Paradox of change

Whenever I think of coping with change, my thoughts almost inevitably turn to my grandmother. Born in 1897 in a tiny house built by her gold-prospecting father, her life was remarkable because it accompanied the growth of her home town. When she was born, it was just a small South African mining town, now it's the sprawling metropolis of Johannesburg. Raised under the harsh and somewhat dusty conditions of a town in its infancy, her life spanned the changes of a century we're still in awe of today.

When my brother and I were little we loved the stories my grandmother told. Her early family life was such a radical departure from our own we'd beg her to tantalise our imaginations with the amazing contrasts of her life. Just when we were enjoying the reality of a man landing on the moon, she would tell us how her British father had taken to the seas in search of his fortune. The boat he arrived in amounted to little more than a crowded tub and his journey from the UK to Australia and then South Africa took over six months. Only three generations later we thought, 'All that time just to go halfway round the world when even the moon can now be reached in just a few days!'

Also while I was foolishly fantasising about handsome princes, she'd tell us how her own mother – on a flimsy promise of marriage – had travelled from England alone. Along with a similarly tedious boat trip, this upright and proper Englishwoman also endured a bumpy 1 500 km stage-coach ride through Africa's rather unwelcoming and dangerous bushveld.

As we cruised along smoothly in our new family sedan, the necessity for such discomfort was almost impossible to fathom – particularly when we considered our own motor car had only rolled off the production line some seventy years later. But as the generation that bridged no-tech and hi-tech, my grandmother made her own choices. As far as motor cars where concerned, she enjoyed the ride but didn't perceive the need to learn to drive herself. She also never ventured into an aeroplane. Even still, she accepted the most amazing developments of our time as just a normal part of everyday life. Technological change neither frightened nor overwhelmed her.

It's only been a few years since her passing but it still fascinates me that the world she left behind – filled as it is with space-shuttles, laptops and cellphones – was completely unimagined by the little girl born in that simple corrugated-iron house in the early days of Johannesburg. During her life I often wondered how she coped. When I asked her she would simply say, 'It's a bit beyond me now, dear!' and with this quip dismiss any further questions.

Can we ignore IT?

If you're in your nineties, this is probably a most appropriate response. But for those of us who aren't quite there yet, putting our head in the sand won't help us take control of our own lives. I suspect my grandmother probably coped because she could sit on the sidelines and watch the technological evolution unfurl from a comfortable distance. It didn't faze her because she invited the things she wanted into her life and rejected those she didn't. But today our reality is different. To manage now we can't pretend it's 'all a bit beyond us' because every day we collide with one new development or another. We can fight technological progress or fear it but neither response alters the fact that the electronic explosion is changing the very fabric of our lives.

Even in our short lifetimes, technology has dramatically shifted our reality. I can clearly remember the day my father brought home one of the earliest electronic calculators. It was a large and cumbersome device, but as children we were staggered by its ability to magically add, subtract and multiply. We whooped with joy because for us it meant the end of tedious multiplication tables! Now only a short thirty years later, we work with powerful computers ten times smaller and a thousand per cent smarter than that old-fashioned and rather clumsy calculator. These machines have added much more than answering simple 9 × 8 questions and the reality is we can no longer ignore them nor keep them at a distance. With a few waves of the electronic wand, technology has deeply penetrated our existence. It has changed what we do for fun, how we interact with each other and the way we'll grow and work in future.

To keep control we try in vain to master the machines. But realistically it's only possible to cope by understanding and mastering the change technology has produced in ourselves. Today the moment a new electronic magician is born, we accept it's already a fossil; but, it's also important to realise that redundancy is not limited to the equipment. Now, more so than ever before, each decade of new development makes a dramatic impact on our thinking and therefore our way of life. The pace we live at is directly linked to technological change and it makes the 'rat-race' of the past look like it was being run by the proverbial tortoise!

IT COLLIDES WITH LIFE

Our beliefs, values and opinions, previously rooted in generations of cultural history, are also fast being rewritten by what we experience around us. For instance, not so long ago it was frowned upon to keep hopping from one job to another. Now in one lifetime it's thought we'll not only have many jobs but these will be wrapped up in five different careers. In just a few fleeting decades we've had to consider and adapt to new ways of living that are very different to the patterns of our parents' past.

Think about how many people you know who are successfully running their second, third or fourth career. My father had three jobs in a single career; but already I have switched career once and great friends of mine are well into their second – even third – professions. Some have moved from the extremes of mining engineering to advertising and others from teaching to sales and then into mainstream business. A good friend started in production and is now successfully running a software consultancy; and another swapped her career in radiology for a life of teaching alternative therapies. A lawyer I know was so despondent in the legal world he switched to journalism; and a friend who was a professional actress studied in midlife to become a successful consulting analyst.

Clearly the whirlwind of change predicted by authors like Alvin Toffler is upon us; and with life being steadily prodded on by technology, 'future shock' is our reality now. Today our world is full of surprises and the only guarantee is to expect there are many more to come. For example, technology has given us more personal freedom and employers are currently making this a reality by downsizing. They are doing so because big companies can't shift fast enough to meet rapidly changing market demand. For us this means many current employees will soon become technically unemployed. This trend reveals that a salary at month-end only provides a false sense of security and as such we're forced to depend more on ourselves. What we can do or produce is fast becoming the only security we have.

Clearly the old structures are collapsing and concepts like the home-office or the flattening of corporate structures are but a few indications of this process. In reality they are creating more equal opportunities for all. The Internet and its ability to share all manner of information rapidly is another way of empowering us. Consumer movements and political protests too are breaking down old systems. They show we're taking back control. But for those who are poorly prepared for greater independence, these trends are precisely what makes progress so scary.

Our natural response to change is to run for cover. But now there's nowhere to hide and worse still progress is robbing us of the comfort of our excuses. We can no longer say: 'My boss (husband or whoever) kept me from being successful' or 'The government must do something about it.' Information technology has made us IT and unless we take full responsibility, living with fear is going to be as good as it gets. Clearly we can no longer rely upon the security of our crumbling social structures. Now we must create stability within ourselves and the only way we can do so is by learning more self-reliance.

TECHNOLOGY'S THRUST: PERSONAL EXPLORATION

So although it could be said that technology may have distanced us from our human nature, paradoxically, it's also pushing us to explore more of ourselves. This message comes across loud and clear when, from time-to-time, an annoying power cut leaves us stranded. Without energy to power our electronic support system, life stops. We can't work, enjoy a great meal, relax in front of the TV or even get in and out of our homes. It's frustrating because no matter how many electronic comforts we have, power cuts are stark reminders we're human.

The issues we're facing were clearly driven home to me when recently my husband and I were out doing our regular but frantic grocery shop in the middle of a pressurised week. Racing back home to our respective appointments, he made a very pertinent comment: 'The problem with life today,' he said, 'is we humans haven't evolved as fast as technology has progressed around us.' And he's a computer whizz, so he's right at the coalface of change!

In other species great changes to the environment bring all sorts of physical adaptations. Mice wrongly introduced to an island close to the Antarctic are growing darker coats to absorb more heat. Now more of them are surviving the freezing winters. Soon they are expected to take over the island. Germs mutate to cheat the efficacy of powerful antibiotics; and some insects have over time adapted to escape the massacre of pesticides.

Yet as human beings we've tried to do the opposite. We've forced the environment to adapt to ourselves. But nature too is full of surprises. Just keeping our heads above the water puts us under constant pressure for evermore intellectual development. We need to keep pushing mental barriers while striving to get smarter. And smarter we've become. Physically we've conquered many of our liabilities and now with new diseases like AIDS we've had to get smarter yet. Intellectually the boundaries keep creeping outwards and the electronic wizards respond by producing new gizmos every day. I have to say, I wouldn't comfortably cope without my technologically driven motor car, dishwasher, smart card or PC but – by trying to force nature to adapt to ourselves – we've also created an environment we find uncomfortable to live in. Now we must evolve to cope with our own creation.

THE NEXT FRONTIER: THE HUMAN SPIRIT

Over the decades the steady flow of innovation has masked the reality that physically and emotionally we haven't changed that dramatically. We have many more tools now but in essence we're not markedly different from the Neanderthals preceding us. It almost borders on the ridiculous to imagine thrusting today's technology upon these early human beings! The result would of course be disastrous. But just considering it provides important clues as to how we can adapt to our new circumstances. Neanderthals may have had fewer tools but they survived because they were more in touch with both themselves and the world around them. So instead of trying to manage our modern-day toys, exploring the human spirit is our next frontier.

This is an important issue because some stability is essential if we're to cope with the ever-increasing pace of change. Given today's reality, we'll only find this security in ourselves. It'll take going full circle and, like our ancestors, we must get back to addressing our fundamental human needs. These are our physical, emotional, mental and spiritual requirements. All four work as a system which when balanced makes us happy. Balance here is a very simple concept. It means making sure our real needs are met. This releases our natural energy which is our source of personal power; and being happy is the key that unlocks this life-force within us.

Yet if we examine technology's influence, it's easy to see how progress has demanded an overemphasis of our intellectual capacity. Academic qualifications, money, status and the desire for lots of worldly possessions have eclipsed our physical, emotional and spiritual energy. If you doubt this, ask yourself whether you're any happier or healthier than your parents were or theirs before them. We may be wealthier or more intellectual but our stressful lifestyle plays havoc with our health and interferes with most of our relationships. It even confuses our needs. While out shopping the other day I happened to overhear someone in all seriousness say, 'What I really need is a new pair of boots!' This tendency to confuse our needs and wants is a symptom of being out of balance. If our real needs aren't being fed, we mistakenly believe a new pair of boots will make us feel better.

HOLISTIC HELP

Consumerism has tipped the balance, so it's not surprising that as it peaked in the eighties we saw the enthusiastic pursuit of health and fitness; and in the nineties a rapid rise in all manner of spiritual followings is evident. It's also no coincidence that the technological explosion fuelled a parallel interest in holism.

Although the term was coined in 1926 by a South African – Jan Smuts – it's only more recently that we're taking a more holistic (or balanced) view of our human system.

As part of this shift much modern science is now dedicated to studying the effect of the mind and emotions on our physical well-being. For example, scientists know that high levels of stress hammer the immune system and, consequently, being out of sorts physically has a direct impact on how we feel emotionally. In many medical establishments – like the now famous Menninger Foundation – links are also being made between incidents of cancer and a lifetime of suppressing destructive feelings, such as anger.

Here I was interested to discover the work of a Harvard Medical School doctor, Herbert Benson. He is studying how the mystifying power of the human spirit makes a critical contribution to our physical health. In his work *Timeless Healing* he refers to the belief in a higher power as a force that helps the healing process. Clearly there is a complex relationship between our physical, emotional, mental and spiritual parts and understanding this means we can get our needs met, we can release our natural source of energy or power. Even though technology may sometimes make us feel helpless, if we manage our power we can take charge of our own lives – no matter what is happening around us.

MANAGING POWER

Take a look at the diagram *below* and imagine that all four areas (physical, emotional, mental and spiritual) add up to 100% of your power. Remember, power means energy and you have a continual supply. What's relevant is that the spiritual is the only source capable of generating power but it's managed by our emotional lives. (Please note when I talk about the spiritual I'm not necessarily referring to religion but more to an individual perception about what gives meaning to your life.) We know the spiritual generates our life-force because when we die our physical body remains but the energy driving it is gone. Also, anyone who's been through a profound spiritual experience reports great surges of power. We know too our emotions manage this force because when we feel good we're energetic.

However, the physical and mental components do not generate power, they consume it. If you recall the last time you studied for an exam, you'll remember how too much mental stimulation is tiring. Even the fittest person is eventually exhausted by continuous physical exertion. So when it comes to the mind and body, the best we can do is to ensure we're not wasting power. If we use our intellect for personal growth and maintain good healthy habits we can conserve it. Both keep us feeling good and this sense of happiness tops up these areas with powerful spiritual energy.

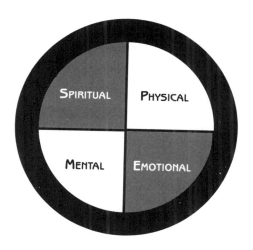

POWER DIAGRAM

To understand the workings of your own energy, think about an average day and calculate how your power is distributed. Write these percentages down. If, for example, you're using a lot of power to manage a challenging career, give yourself a high percentage – let's say 70 % – in the mental quadrant. Then distribute the remaining 30 % according to how you use your energy in the other three areas. Sticking with this example, if the majority of your energy is already dedicated to one area, how are you going to manage the demands of your physical, emotional and spiritual life? Let's explore it.

After a mentally exhausting day you get home and your spouse and children want some of your time and energy. You however want to go to the gym. Already low on energy, you become ratty and short-tempered. This consumes more energy but you also start losing power over the emotional grapple between your own wants versus your family's needs. Eventually you give up on the gym and slump into exhaustion. Now operating on a nett energy loss, what's left to meet your other needs? I bet not even enough to console yourself and less still to ponder the mysteries of life!

Puncture Prevention

What prevents such a loss of energy is the ability to manage your power from an emotional and spiritual perspective. This you'll learn in chapters 3 and 8 respectively. What's important for now is that although these two areas generate and manage your power, you can experience losses in all four areas. This happens when you're not in control of your life. So energy losses are due to the choices you make.

EXAMPLES OF ENERGY DRAINS

PHYSICAL	MENTAL
Addictions (alcohol, cigarettes, drugs)	Boredom/stagnation
Ill health/physical pain	Complaining
Insufficient sleep	Guilt
Lack of exercise	Negative thinking
Lack of relaxation	Stress
Poor eating habits	Worry

EMOTIONAL	**SPIRITUAL**

Controlling other people

Dependency (allowing others to control you)

Emotional outbursts

Fear

Fights, arguments

Inability to manage your own emotions

Not getting your own way

Lack of discipline

Lack of faith

Lack of trust

Life with no meaning nor purpose

Poor quality time

Energy losses reduce the 100% capacity. So you may want to go back to your percentages and correct them to better reflect these choices that drain your life-force. Are you possibly beginning to get a grip on why you feel so drained, stressed or down? But more importantly, these energy patterns also have an impact upon the events in your life. A lack of physical power translates into poor health. Either you may be experiencing this currently or are heading for a health crisis in future. Likewise, if you have no emotional energy to spare, your relationships will at best be unsatisfying, at worst calamitous. Losses in the mental area will affect your ability to achieve and no spiritual energy means no life fulfilment. These are reflected in the diagram *below*.

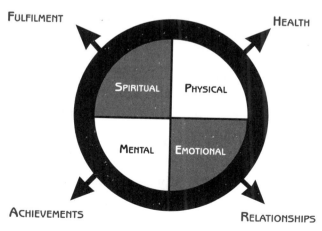

SYMPTOMS OF ENERGY DRAINS

SUCCESS IS ENERGY

So as said by the inspiring author Carolyn Myss in her book *Why People Don't Heal and How They Can*, life is about managing your energy – your personal power. The better you are at it, the happier and more successful you can become. It's about disciplining yourself to do the things that feed your system and putting a stop to those that drain you. Continual growth, good-quality relationships, physical health and fitness maintain your personal power; and being happy, having a meaningful vision as well as faith in yourself, life and your God feed it.

These are the things happy and successful people focus on. That's why they seem to have more energy. They aren't especially gifted or even any stronger or more intelligent than you are. They're just better at using their will to manage their lives. When your will-power manages how you live physically, emotionally, mentally and spiritually, the truth is you can be happy and successful too.

The diagram on page 13 illustrates how your will-power or self-discipline is like a cement wall retaining your energy. But like any dam wall it takes only a few serious leaks to pull the plug on the whole system. Personal crises cause major leakages, but self-discipline goes a long way to prevent them. This book will teach you the discipline necessary to manage your energy. It'll show you what you're doing that drains power and teach you how to channel power back into your own life success.

As you retrieve your personal power you'll find the process both exciting and exhilarating. But it will require change. So when you're working through it, don't be lured by technology's illusion. Unlike technological innovation, personal change doesn't happen overnight. It's more like the grind of making filter coffee rather than marginally satisfying your desire with a cup of instant! You also have to make it yourself. Buying books or going on seminars can inspire you, but nothing will change unless you actively apply the disciplines to your life.

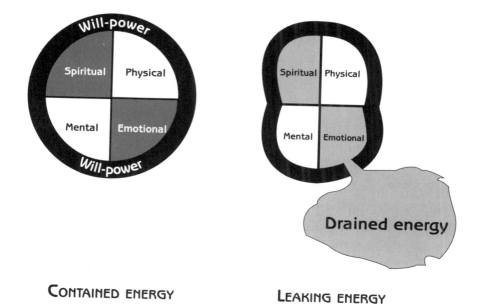

CONTAINED ENERGY   LEAKING ENERGY

CHOOSE CHANGE

Sure, change is hard and I've often heard it said that we fear change more than we fear death itself. But like it or not, our world is demanding that we change and now our survival is dependent upon it. Our old habits apply to structures that are crumbling and if we continue stubbornly to resist change, we'll collapse along with them. Think about it. Many people still work from nine to five. One wonders why. We lose energy hustling traffic to reach crowded offices, forgetting technology has made them obsolete. We waste time talking about the hours we work and the stress we endure as if they're virtues but fail to see the value of this work-ethic died a long time ago. Then our aspirations keep our weekends filled with bustling malls as we frantically pursue bigger and better goods to fortify how we feel. Even more ridiculous, we use up our remaining energy complaining because life isn't as it was. It's so absurd! We'd rather lose power than choose to change. Instead of wasting our life-force clinging to old habits, perhaps we'd be better off shifting our perspective.

Here putting technology into perspective is vital to our happiness because if we're scared of the impact it's having, we lose power. But the fact is technology exists to make life easier. From a physical point of view it's supposed to save time not overwhelm us. Instead of having to slaughter our own meat, make candles and soap, we have more freedom if we learn to get our needs met in other ways. The Internet, fax machines and cellphones make it possible for us to work from a beach in the Caribbean or at home. Yet we still cling to our offices to satisfy our social and emotional needs. So if we learn to choose differently, instead of being bundled with co-workers we may or may not like, we can now elect to be around the people who feed our soul.

Technology has also made information accessible. It supports our continual growth. Now at the push of a button anyone can explore knowledge from all corners of the globe. We can get information about motor mechanics or meditation, take university degrees or observe Mars without ever leaving home. By removing the mundane, it has given us the freedom to learn new skills as well as the information, time and tools to explore our emotional and spiritual possibilities. We're not at the mercy of its rapid pace nor are we its victims. When we use it to fuel our system we change the relationship: we become the master and technology our slave.

Technology won't however do it for us. To adapt, we need to choose new ways of living, thinking, working and being. This book will help you do so. Be aware that just reading the information is not enough. The success of the programme requires implementing the thinking every day. Like thousands of other people who've applied this material, you too can use the tools to develop more rewarding life habits. These will help you unleash the power to cope with change and uncover your great potential for success. Use this book to create whatever you want to achieve.

As you are working through it, bear in mind that this programme is not about self-improvement. Remember right now you are as perfect as you're ever going to be. You were made that way. As such you already have all the talents, gifts and goodness of life inside of you. However if your life isn't working perfectly, this doesn't mean you have some inherent flaw in your make-up. It only means you haven't yet learnt to manage your unlimited power successfully. It's the only imperfection you may have. Use this book to find personal management tools that can assist you to discover and become the person you really are.

Success myths
debunked

Ever since I can remember, the concept of 'success' has been shrouded in mystery. At some point or other we've all been fed the line that we won't succeed because we're not clever enough, don't work hard enough, aren't well connected or are insufficiently educated. Whatever it takes, apparently most people don't have enough of it! Although there's a shred of truth in this, it's not what we've been told. Success translates into power and those who have it are in control. In times past either the physically strong took command or the spiritually superior dominated. Now in our own westernised cultures control has become a mind game. It translates into knowledge + money = power and this simple equation has given rise to many unfounded myths about what it takes to be successful.

But life is changing rapidly; and like it or not, information technology is the central player making us more equal. Now anyone who can access the Internet has free passage to planetary knowledge that was previously jealously guarded by a few. Also the growing middle class means that for the first time more people have more money than ever before. Both these factors give us greater independence and this is causing an interesting shift in the seat of power. Now the important question is 'Who is in control?'

Those who previously ruled by virtue of their social standing are being ousted by those who are willing to take responsibility for themselves. If you break up the word 'responsibility' to read 'response-ability' you'll see that it simply means being able to respond. It boils down to how you invest your energy. Now with the greater freedom provided by technology and money, many people are making some striking new choices. They're no longer blindly following external forms of control and are putting a stop to other people – like those in governments, businesses or cultures – dictating how they should respond. So instead of others having power over you, the world is shifting to more internal forms of self-control.

The fact that the Australian Rupert Murdoch controls Britain's media, physically disabled Stephen Hawkins dominates science, the Egyptian Mohammed Al-Fayad heads up Harrods and Anita Roddick owns and controls The Body Shop globally shows a new direction. The glass ceilings imposed by class, race and gender are slowly disintegrating and some of the most significant beliefs about success are shattering with them. This is a clear indication that investing your personal power wisely is more important than the way you look or where you were born. Now it's up to you to replace these illusions with more personal control.

SUCCESS MYTHS CRUMBLE

These growing trends have also led to a re-think about what it takes to be successful. Now modern research has shown that correlating achievement to intellect or education has too become redundant. Daniel Goleman in his groundbreaking work *Emotional Intelligence* turned this fable around when he revealed that success is a reward for having learnt high levels of emotional and social skills. It's not about university degrees or intellectual ability. In fact, emotional dexterity comprises 80% of the factors contributing to success and IQ has become its poor cousin. It can account only for the remaining percentage.

Simply put, emotional intelligence is emotional maturity or the emotional quotient (EQ as it's better known). It's about how well we manage our energy or power and it's easy to relate to. We know that when we're overwhelmed by a foul mood it's hard to confront the challenges we face and even harder still to get others to co-operate with our plans. But if we can manage ourselves, life is easier to cope with and so are our relationships. Goleman is quite clear on the point that those who have a high level of EQ are more likely to master life's ups and downs than those with a high IQ but few life-skills.

EQ makes a lot of sense when considered in the context of emotions managing our life-force or power. By bringing this thinking out into the open, Goleman has given the world a great gift. He has overturned the unfounded conviction that IQ and academia are the principal route to success. It's a potent belief that has been popular since the forties and it's kept many would-be achievers from fulfilling their potential. I know one such talented fellow who was married to a friend of mine. Today in his late fifties he's likely to land up on the streets. So strong is his belief in academic qualifications that without a university degree he's been unable to secure a career for himself. As he's obviously talented he lands jobs here and there, but inevitably he lets his educational inadequacy strip him of his power and he fails.

I've heard of many others like him, but now with Goleman's research showing us how transparent this potent illusion is, perhaps tragedies like these needn't happen again. Based on his work today, we can confidently say that anyone with even a relatively average IQ has the power to succeed. Along with the contribution that technology has made to levelling the playing fields, this new thinking is exciting because it brings more E-Quality to our lives.

STREET TEST EQ

If you have any doubts about this, put EQ to the test. Consider the children you were at school with. Who succeeded later in life? Were they the ones who typically got the highest grades or do our success stories today emerge more often from those who were average scholastic performers? Although there are exceptions, most of my peers who are successful now are those who scraped through school but learnt many other valuable life-skills along the way. Obviously this doesn't mean top grades will lead to failure later in life. This would be a ludicrous claim. Nevertheless, the important message from Goleman's work is that having a high IQ is no guarantee for success in adult life. Clearly social and emotional skills are more valuable than intellectual ability.

In a conversation with Maureen – a delegate on one of my seminars – she was astounded to see how accurately this thinking had played out in her life. Maureen had been the model child and her friend was the street-wise rebel. After leaving school she entered full-time study and her pal went straight into business. Today, armed with a masters degree, she is the communications manager for a large corporate company, her friend the CEO.

Now this isn't to say that college is a waste of time, but the problem arises if, like Maureen, you rely upon it as the sole contributor to your success. Sure if you want to be a medical practitioner you'll need to study the workings of the human body. However, having such a degree won't necessarily make you a good doctor.

In business today academic qualifications are even less important. This happens more in the commercial world than anywhere else where it's not unusual for high-achieving adults to have been rebellious children at school. Their grades may have been shoddy, but their mischief taught them to stand on their own two feet emotionally. Often you'll hear parents moaning about the woes of rebellious children. Understandably they fear drugs, unruly gang behaviour, runaways and unwanted pregnancies. Of course today these are very real concerns.

Yet much of this destructive behaviour is a way for children to escape the demands of controlling, pushy parents. Rebellious children are expressing the need to manage their own power and what many parents don't see is that inappropriate behaviour is more likely to happen when children aren't involved in decisions about their lives. Teenagers especially are looking for love and attention for who they are, not for what they do or are likely to become. Now that we know that high grades don't necessarily produce good entrepreneurs, teachers, lawyers or business managers, we can get off our children's backs and help them to learn some of the more helpful life-skills as they grow.

YOU HAVE SOMETHING SPECIAL

This is vital because the interesting thing about human nature is that every one of us has the power to be something special. No matter where you were born, who raised you, where you went to school or how well you did or didn't do, each of us has the gifts or talents necessary to fulfil a unique purpose in life. And we all have one: it's known as your life-work. It's about living to the fullest, being the very best that you can be and it doesn't matter what you do. 'Always remember,' an analyst once told me, 'we're human beings, not human doings!'

I've heard many people complain about self-help courses and books because trainers and authors assume that everyone has a burning desire to be tremendously successful. Here it's important to understand that success is a very individual matter. Contrary to what we see around us, it's not only about gathering lots of wealth and many possessions along the way. To prominent people like Nelson Mandela and the late Mahatma Gandhi, things other than money were more meaningful measures of their achievements. Needless to say, this doesn't diminish the accomplishments of many hundreds of successful billionaires, it just shows that their needs are different. So it really doesn't matter on which side of the spectrum your aspirations fall; all that success means is moulding yourself into the person you want to be. The more valid question is 'Do you know what you want and are you prepared to go out and get it?'

Many people grapple with this and it's usually because of yet another success myth that we're plugged into. People who haven't discovered what they want struggle because they think that there's nothing extraordinary about them. But it doesn't matter whether we're talking about Gandhi or Bill Gates, the strange thing about these and other successful people is that they didn't start with any unusual gifts or privileges. At the beginning of their careers they were ordinary people, no more talented than you or me.

For example, the great Mahatma launched his career as a shy and very mediocre lawyer. Early in his life he went to South Africa where, from the moment he stepped onto dry soil, the racial injustices infuriated him. Instead of succumbing, he used his fury to unleash his passion and harnessed this powerful energy to mobilise the local Indian population. The experiences and successes he had while resisting oppression in South Africa were built upon and used ultimately to overturn British rule in India.

Yes, Gandhi was a gifted man. But the gifts that he had are lodged in all of us. The difference between people like the Mahatma and the average person is that Gandhi used his experiences to unleash his rare brand of talent. Every step of his journey was a step towards greater personal and spiritual growth; and the more he progressed, the more powerful he became. We'll never know, but perhaps if he'd not had those early experiences he may have continued to live as a mediocre lawyer and died a frustrated man. Millions of gifted people exist like this. But for you the truth is that if you release your passion and channel it in a disciplined way, you too can achieve whatever you want. Like Gandhi, it takes exercising your will-power to gain control of your mind, and you'll discover how to do this in the next few chapters.

THE GIFT OF EXPERIENCE

When it comes to finding out what's extraordinary about you, you'll need to start with the gifts you've been given. One of the main difficulties with this is that many people can't think of a single talent they have. I know this because lots of my seminar delegates say so and for me it's a sad reality that such a large percentage of people believe that they have no talents at all. They think that when gifts were being handed out their particular talent vendor was on lunch! Yet it's not true. It's a false self-perception. Every human being has so many abilities that we're never likely to explore all our gifts in one lifetime. The problem is never a lack of gifts. It's only a lack of experience.

Our experiences show us who we are and what we're capable of; and each new circumstance is an opportunity to decide how we invest our power. It's as simple as determining whether we can or can't deal with the situation. But the consequences are more profound. Every time you say, 'This is too much for me, I can't handle it,' you pull the plug on your system. This drains the energy from you and makes you helpless to change the situation. Even if you're filled with talent, you will no longer have the energy to fire your special gifts into action. So rather than being the master of your own destiny, you become the victim of your choices.

Yet the interesting thing is that very ordinary people who've used their experiences to boost their growth are making front-page news today. Like them, if we persist, problems push us to dig deep into our talent bag to unearth the stuff that we're really made of. Challenges expose our natural gifts because every issue that we resolve helps us discover that we may be stronger or more creative than we initially thought. This learning strengthens our emotional equipment; and the more sophisticated our tools are, the better geared we are to solve more complex problems in the future. Only by learning about ourselves do we build the kind of confidence necessary to manage each stage of opportunity as we progress.

I'll illustrate this by using an extreme example. It doesn't matter how gifted some children are, it would be disastrous if they skipped school and went straight to university. Even if they had the IQ of a genius, they wouldn't have sufficient experience to cope with the opportunity they'd been given. Likewise, Pavarotti didn't begin by performing to audiences of thousands and Abe Lincoln didn't become president overnight. If they had, neither would have coped. So believing that the luck-of-the draw makes some people successful is just another myth.

LUCK OR PLUCK?

High achievers build their luck by learning from their experiences; and the braver they become, the more opportunities they're able to seize. Of course success takes courage, but what few people have grasped is that everybody has lots of it. Discover how much you have by pitting yourself against your experiences. Once you do you'll notice that the more pluck you have the luckier you become. Magic happens when we back our natural talent with a confident belief in our ability to overcome. So, if you've been waiting for a genie to conjure up your life's wishes, you'll discover it by looking inside yourself.

Therefore, the more experiences you've had – regardless of whether you've labelled them good or bad – the more opportunities you've had to build your emotional resources. It's no secret that this is how normal people grow to be exceptionally successful. They turn what may initially seem to be insurmountable obstacles into valuable stepping stones along the way. And the truth is that if you use your experiences to learn more about who you are, there's no reason why you shouldn't

23

join the ranks of these highly successful people. Start now by thinking about some of the major obstacles you've had to overcome. What did they teach you about your capabilities or emotional endurance?

Not having strong emotional resources is like trying to tune a motor car with the plastic tools that you played with as a child. If you don't have the right equipment, you'll be standing at the roadside clutching your phoney hammer while the opportunities drive by. You'll probably just see them as motor cars rather than each one representing a chance for you to express who you want to become. It's really what growing up was all about. Things that floored you as a child don't faze you now because you've got the tools to deal with them. Of course success also takes other qualities like passion, commitment, determination and persistence, but no one was born with these traits. These qualities are disciplines that successful people have grown into along the way. Everyone can learn to apply their will-power to channel natural energy into their own success. This book will show you how.

GROWTH: INSTINCT OR CHOICE?

Your personal power exists to boost growth. There's no shortcut when it comes to success. In its simplest form it's like putting a jigsaw puzzle together. Every step that we take, whether we succeed or fail, gives us another meaningful piece of information to put together the picture of who we are now and who we want to become. This point is critical because growth and learning are part of our natural instinct to survive.

If our ancestors hadn't learnt about poisonous plants, wild animals or nature's uncertain temperament, we definitely would not be here to tell the tale. This instinctive need to grow lives on in us; it can be seen from a very early age by watching a baby learning to sit up, crawl or walk. No one needs to teach infants these skills. Instinct powers their motivation. Even when it's obviously a frustrating process, a baby will never give up; it will never stop trying until the next stage has been mastered.

Our potential for achievement is embodied in this instinctive need for growth, but as adults our minds and emotions can interfere with this natural motivator. Nevertheless, whenever we solve a problem, make sense of an issue or are stimulated by something new, we feel its energy working. So, if you're able to say that you are actively participating in your own growth right now, then you're already tapping into this winning energy. The next step is to continue exploring your assets and this will keep you growing into your extraordinary potential.

To stick with this process you need to understand that, like a baby learning to walk, trying new steps takes persistence, patience and time. This applies whether we're talking about getting our needs met, uncovering more of our talents and gifts or following our natural instinct to grow. You may say, 'Well that's all well and fine, but in the hurly-burly of our modern world the one thing that we're fast running out of is time.'

THE MIRACLE OF MORE TIME

Yes, the reality of the pace at which we live means that our personal ambitions, goals or careers often clash with family demands. It's also inevitable that the DIY job on the plumbing becomes more urgent than reading a book to feed your soul. Then fetching and carrying kids – while juggling the shopping, cooking and cleaning – takes priority over spending fulfilling time with your spouse. And in-between catching a fleeting movie or relaxing in front of the TV, we cram in a few hurried moments for a social life! Of course it's already too much! But if success is what you want you're going to need to make more time: more time for you.

You can achieve this seemingly impossible feat if you understand that the problem is not really how you manage your time, but more how you manage your choices. In reality the range of choices that you have is unlimited. To come to terms with your behaviour ask yourself at the end of each day, 'Why do I make the choices I do?' Is it a habit to listen to other people complaining or is it just a waste of time? Did your choices meet your needs or were you too busy fulfilling others' demands? Time is an issue because it's about how you invest your energy, so questioning your choices is therefore vital to managing your time.

Is success scary?

Questioning your decisions reveals your habits and priorities. It shows where you place your power and reveals there's good reason for everything that you do. If you're wondering why you waste so much time, it could be a defence to cover up some of your fears. It may sound strange, but many people are deeply afraid of success and they're scared for a number of reasons. The most common is that success may destroy them and in our society this is not an unfounded concern. We've made a habit of supporting people on their way up and then crucifying them when they get to the top of the pile. Princess Diana, John Lennon and River Phoenix were all victims of this. That's why learning emotional strength from our experiences is so important. Although it's not bullet-proof it at least cushions the blows and so makes us immune to harsh opinions.

A second popular reason for fearing success is envy. Many people are concerned that envious friends may fall by the wayside. I hate to break the bad news, but this is often quite true. I know a very successful self-made entrepreneur whom people in another city across the country hate – and they've never even met him! Yes it's crazy, but if this is happening to you, deal with it in one of two ways. Sure it's easy to take this stuff personally, but it's also a great acknowledgement of your achievement. One way will sink you, the other will boost your confidence. You choose.

The third reason is best revealed by a quote from Nathaniel Branden in his book *How to Raise Your Self-Esteem*. He asks: 'Why is it that people would rather be miserable than be happy and successful?' This issue raises questions about how we perceive our responsibilities and of course your success will change them. Again it's your call. But would you rather live with the burden of poverty or be able to respond to the happiness and freedom of success?

When it comes down to it, human beings have an enormous potential for happiness and feeling successful is the fodder that fuels it. Here I don't necessarily mean cavorting through life doing cartwheels every day. That's manic! Rather happiness is about feeling content, being comfortable with what's happening in your life right now. In a practical sense it's about knowing that you have the power to deal with change, challenges, mistakes, failures and successes along the way. But, more importantly, as happiness releases our life-force, it's the state of mind that makes all else possible.

So success has nothing to do with social standing, education level, IQ or luck. These are just excuses that we use to cover the low-grade choices we're in the habit of making. But if success is what you truly want then heed this passage from the Bible that says: 'Keep your heart with all diligence, for out of it spring the issues of life' (*Proverbs* 4:23). Being emotionally robust means being able to drink abundantly from this spring and now, with more E-Quality, anyone can develop the tools to do this. 'Keeping your heart with diligence' is the key and this will be fully explored in the next chapter.

The grammar of
our emotions

Over the years much of the personal growth literature supports the fact that we were born to win. Nature is loaded with life's winning ways and we are no exception. Whenever seeds successfully grow into plants, when the earth completes its annual orbit around the sun and even when our human cells silently regenerate themselves for our health and well-being, we experience nature's miraculous power working. Nature is geared for mastery and this built-in potential for success is life's greatest gift to us. It's the most exciting birthday present we'll ever get. Inside the wonderful wrapping of our physical form are all the ingredients just waiting to be moulded successfully into whatever we want. These tools are our emotional, mental, and spiritual assets. While all are covered in this book, we begin with our most under-utilised resource – the energy of our hearts or our emotions.

Emotions make us feel real. They let us know that we're alive, and not a day goes by when we don't feel something. Some days we feel exhilarated, energetic, happy and ready to take on the world. It's a wonderful feeling. We're up and buzzing, getting things done, feeling so capable that nothing's too much for us. Then we also have days when we have to drag ourselves out of bed in the morning. We can all recall those dark and heavy days when even the simplest chores take a lot of effort. Like unpredictable weather, the sunny and blustery moments just seem to come and go, almost as if we've no control over them.

Realistically, feelings are neither unseasonal nor unpredictable. They are deeply ingrained, unconscious emotional habits that administer our power. Personal power is the energy that we use to make sure we get our own way; but how we go about it makes a difference. If we're good at it we tap into healthy life-skills to manoeuvre situations to achieve the outcome we want. This guarantees success. But when we're emotionally inept our feelings are deployed as devious weapons to manipulate other people. We know that this makes our relationships miserable. It also drains our energy. Either way we're expressing learnt emotional habits and these patterns have a powerful influence in shaping our lives.

EMOTION: ROLLERCOASTER OR DRIVING FORCE?

Think of your heart as the chief executive of the power-station generating energy in your system. It operates like an autocratic employer and what our feelings dictate, the mind and body naturally follow. Our hearts feed energy into the mental and physical and that's why feelings determine our movements. The word 'emotion' tells us that this is so. Its stem comes from the Latin phrase *e-motere* meaning 'to move'. We often say that we're 'moved' by a deeply touching experience; but in reality all feelings influence the decisions that parent our actions. Where we live, our career, who our friends are and the interests that we have are all choices we've made based on how we felt at the time – or hoped to feel in future.

So great is the influence of our emotions that our behaviour is driven by our emotional habits; this adds up to our attitude. Have you ever noticed how so many people feel light and happy on a Friday afternoon and heavy again by Monday morning? It's a weekly ritual. Yet the truth is that we're not emotional yo-yos mindlessly swinging between Friday buoyancy and Monday blues. In reality neither time nor other people have control over the seasons of our feelings – only we do.

Once we learn to manage our emotions we need never live at the mercy of our moods. This is a critical issue in learning to 'keep our hearts with diligence' because we know that when we're sour and surly we're seldom productive. We also know that we're unpleasant to be around. Many talented individuals have been toppled from high positions because they made the mistake of keeping tight control over others rather than taking charge of themselves. Whenever we trade self-mastery for power over other people, those who could give us a helping hand end up giving us the finger instead!

It's a wise person who understands that we can't be success-ful alone. Whether we like it or not, all achievements involve help, support, ideas, information or even money from others; and if we want their co-operation, we must learn self-control. This is an essential ingredient for success because control stops our moods from interfering with our relationships. It's a key issue in becoming more emotionally intelligent. So to raise our level of EQ we must first address some of our deeply ingrained emotional habits.

SOCIALISED IMMATURITY

As children, girls and boys are taught to cope with their emotions differently. Traditionally daughters were taught to express socially acceptable feelings and suppress those that were not. For sons, 'cowboys don't cry' meant that the rational was prioritised over the emotional and boys learnt to ignore their feelings. Neither habit is healthy.

Talking about our emotions does no more than let off a little steam; and stifling them bottles things up. Both silence our true feelings and we know that stifled emotions behave like children who've been scolded. They act out with tantrums and tears at the most inappropriate times. So keeping a lid on our emotions only provides a thin veneer that shouldn't be confused with true self-control.

Self-control is about understanding the power of feelings and using them to get accurate information about our lives. This thinking differs greatly from the emotional habits we picked up in childhood. But by learning to handle our feelings differently, these new tools mean that we can stop banging our heads against the same emotional brick wall.

However – be prepared – developing more mature habits involves continually testing these new practices against your experiences. It requires lots of learning and here you'll have to accept that change isn't going to happen overnight. The techniques are easier than you think, but you'll need to keep working at them.

POWERFUL SOURCE OF INFORMATION

Learning to deal with our feelings is the first step because how we manage our emotions determines how we use our energy, or power. Feelings do much more than simply add a touch of spice. They provide a constant stream of information that translates and decodes what's happening to us. If used appropriately, this feedback empowers us.

The valuable information provided by our feelings interprets our experiences and profoundly influences our perception of reality. You and I can be in the same situation, but it may make you happy while I'm angry and frustrated. With such conflicting experiences, we may just as well have been in two different circumstances.

We're at odds because our feelings decide the value of our experiences. Happiness tells you that the event was good for you. It was worthwhile. My feelings tell me the opposite. Neither is right nor wrong: it's just the way our feelings help us to discover who we are.

FEELINGS COMMUNICATE

Feelings make sense of our lives because essentially they are messages. They come from the deepest part of our soul and speak to us about what we want. As the source of such vital information, it's important to accept that you have a right to all of your feelings. In the above example you could tell me that I'm overreacting or being silly and unfair, but it won't alter the way that I feel.

Similarly, I can't change your reaction and blaming you for upsetting me gives me nothing to work with. Only by accepting my right to be angry can I make sense of this important information. My anguish is telling me something – either I must change my attitude or move away from this unhappy situation.

Feelings move us using a language of their own, and to understand it we must learn the grammar of our emotions. Broadly speaking, emotions can be divided into two categories – love and fear. Light, breezy, positive feelings like joy, happiness and passion are charged with the power of love. Now when I talk about 'love' I'm not referring to the romance of candlelit dinners, red hearts and roses. Love here is seen in the sense of loving life – with all its ups and downs, its taxing and successful moments. On the other hand, emotions such as anger and frustration are fuelled by fear. Lots of people are scared of change, failure, making mistakes, looking foolish or not being good enough. Also, as already discussed, many are equally frightened of being happy and successful.

ENERGY IN MOTION

The distinction between love and fear is important because the two emotions disperse our energy differently. So let's first examine the power of 'loving' energy. When we're in love we know it. It's as if we've been hit by a bolt of lightning and through our rose-tinted view we're deliriously happy, motivated and powerful. The same applies to loving life. It gives us a positive charge and fills us with energy. This makes us constructive, inspired, resourceful and proactive. It also makes us exciting for others to be around. Our feelings release energy because 'e-motion' is simply energy in motion. When we're happy we feel its positive charge and can channel this injection of power into whatever we do. For as long as the feeling lasts we have enough bounce to sustain ourselves.

Happiness is a balanced state of mind. It means that our needs are being met in all four areas; and for us to achieve a good quality of life we need to be cheerful most of the time. Being happy is the only feeling that has the power to liberate our life-force; and by releasing energy it sets up a productive cycle. The more successful we are, the better we feel; and when we feel great we release even more energy. This is what being motivated means.

Practically, it entails using our emotions to guide our decisions so that we stay happy and can keep doing what's right for ourselves. If we consider work to be our adult way of expressing who we are, it makes sense that when we fuel it with the energy of 'loving' what we do then we're likely to be good at it. Knowing this, the fact that 80 % of US employees don't like their jobs is of concern. Imagine how much more successful the country would be if all that energy and creative potential was released into the economy!

GET A MOVE ON!

Motivation is not about hype. It's about how you use your emotional energy and it can only come from within. Although we may believe that we're motivated by quality of life, money, status or power, in reality we're only motivated for two reasons. The first is to create the life that we want and the second is to move away from situations that don't suit us. Manifesting the lifestyle after which you hunger is charged with love. It draws you towards an exciting vision and this feeling releases your energy or life-force. It keeps you moving forward.

The second is motivated by fear and it roots you in the past. You may want to move away, but without a vision or destination you'll have no idea in which direction you're heading. In fact I've heard it described as a bit like driving your motor car using only the rear-view mirror to guide you. You'll probably drift slowly for a while, until eventually you crash into something. This level of motivation is only useful if employed in the right context. For example if you want to give up smoking, fear can be a powerful motivator to get you to stop.

At this point take some time to consider which motivator instigates most of your decisions. The first gives you the oomph to move forward and the second only makes you disgruntled with what you've got. Both are energy in motion, but they produce different results. Love thrusts your life-force into creative activities, but fear drains you – it makes you feel terrible. Worse still, your mind is dragged down by your emotions so your thoughts keep reminding you how incompetent and helpless you are. This saps even more energy. Feeling weak and unable to manage your life, you start withdrawing into yourself. It's a vicious circle and you end up feeling lifeless and lethargic – like an old dishrag hung out to dry.

ALL EMOTIONS ARE OKAY TO FEEL – SOME OF YOUR RESPONSES ARE NOT

But if we learn to tap into the real power of these fear-based emotions, it needn't be this way. Remember that our emotions are messages and that these bad feelings need special attention. Unhappiness is feedback telling you that something's wrong. It's letting you know that you're losing power. So, if you address the attitudes, thoughts or behaviour that are causing unhappiness, you can start retrieving the force that will make you feel good again. Practically this is how it works.

Brenda, a really gentle secretary in a business I consulted to, became so unhappy that she exploded one day when I telephoned.

In a loud, out-of-character voice she was bitching heavily because her work colleagues kept overloading her. 'I'm so fed up,' she said, 'I can't see any way out except to leave.' When I enquired about other areas in her life, her husband, friends and children came under fire too for taking advantage of her.

I asked Brenda why she hadn't put a stop to it and she replied, 'Well, if I don't do these things maybe they'll stop liking me.' So next I queried how likeable she could be when she was so angry and upset – she burst into tears. By working with these bad feelings Brenda slowly understood that her life habit was to trade happiness for popularity. But it always backfired. Now Brenda is growing into saying 'no' and this is helping her to retrieve her energy. As for popularity, the change in her has gained other people's respect. Now they've stopped treating her like the doormat she once pretended to be.

Instead of stewing like Brenda did, you'll make more headway by listening to the messages of your feelings. But you'll have to ask the right sort of questions to get a useful reply. These question our own thoughts, attitudes and behaviour, not the conduct of others. 'What is this feeling telling me?' 'What choices have I made to get here?' 'Why did I make these choices?' 'What's holding me back?' 'What are my options?' Questions like these reveal our unconscious habits and show us how we got into a mess in the first place. Once we know why we made these choices we're free to change our decisions and make better plans for our behaviour in future.

THE LANGUAGE OF EMOTIONS

If you respond appropriately to these fear-based feelings, unhappiness becomes a powerful motivator for change. These feelings are valuable because not only do they put pressure on us to grow, but they also accurately point us in the right direction. In Brenda's case her feelings were urging her to stand her ground and this was the leverage she needed to improve all of her relationships. For her the message came through anger; and like an intricate vocabulary, each different feeling gives us specific information. To gain a deeper understanding of this emotional language you may want to now turn to appendix 1 where a glossary is provided. It's like a dictionary providing you with the meaning of each emotion and it also suggests actions you can take to minimise power losses.

The first thing you're likely to notice is that there are many more fear-based emotions. You'll recall that the foundation of a good life rests on being happy most of the time. So fear-based feelings work like the warning lights in a modern motor car. They tell us when our happiness – the energy that fuels us – is threatened. While driving, a smooth-running engine is reassuring. Being happy works in the same way. It says that our system is running sweetly; we're only warned when our thoughts or behaviours lead us astray. But if we stop and correct the problem, the warning light switches off and the bad feeling subsides.

To illustrate how this works, let's use 'frustration' as an example. Although we do grow and change when we're happy, sometimes our comfort zone gets a little too cosy and complacency is preferable to change. Remember that continual growth is central to our happiness; and by looking up the message of 'frustration' you'll see that it's telling us to move on. Think about the last time that you felt frustrated. What brought you relief? Probably change.

Now this doesn't necessarily mean that if you're suffering Monday blues you need to switch careers or leave town. I know of many people who've mistakenly thrown in the towel, hoping that a new job, city or country will make all the difference. In particular, Penny, a marketing consultant in her late thirties, comes to mind.

When I met her she was already sunk by her frustration. She was visibly anxious, had difficulty sleeping, her relationships were up and down; and in business she was scattered, unable to concentrate on one thing at a time. No matter what, Penny was adamant that her problems would be solved by moving town. Although I urged her to dig deeper into her emotional life, within a few weeks she'd packed up and gone.

For about six months Penny reported that life was great. She was more relaxed, could sleep better and her business seemed to be moving. Then, after the honeymoon period was just about over, the same irritable and disgruntled Penny started creeping back. The glamour of the new city only excited her while she was being challenged to master the change. Now her emotional baggage has caught up with her and she's having to face the real issues once again. Possibly these could include learning to like and respect herself a little more, reviewing some of her relationships or even rethinking the way she does her job. Whatever the case, no new city will make her happy for long.

Pulling the heartstrings

Quick-fix reactions often lead to disappointment; and because of this I usually advise people not to make any physical move until they've learnt to be relatively happy where they are. Although it can happen, it's rare that our emotions signal physical change. More likely they demand that we learn something about ourselves.

Like Penny the problem is that too much of our power is invested in blame and that's why we're often so full of complaints. But the truth is that no one else can respond to how we're feeling; and inflicting our bad reactions on the external world is pointless. It wastes the very thing that we need to address the real problem – energy. The more it leaks, the more helpless we are to change the situation and this is what makes us so unhappy. Instead, if we get into the habit of looking inside ourselves we can start seeing which of our habits or behaviours need to change. We do so by reading the message of our feelings, making the necessary changes and then moving on.

FACE UP TO YOUR FEELINGS

The danger of blaming others or running from unhappiness is that life has an uncanny knack of putting us back into similar situations over and over again. Have you ever noticed how people complain about the same thing all the time? The job or relationship may be different but the stories are always the same. They remind me of Shirley Maclean's great line in the movie *Steel Magnolias*. When Julia Roberts asks her what is wrong, she says, 'Nothing! I've just been in a bad mood for forty years!' These are people who are not being let off the hook by their feelings; and you see them proudly parading their life's slogan on T-shirts saying, 'Same shit. Different day'! If you gripe, think what you're complaining about because these are the areas where you're losing power. Only more energy will make you feel better; so instead of complaining, consider what you should change to recharge the life-force that drives you?

This is important because feelings don't go away unless we deal with the issues causing them. If you look up the meaning of anger in appendix 1, you'll see how this applies. Generally a feeling of anger tells you that you're not getting your own way and are therefore feeling compromised. If you decide that it's your wife who always makes you angry, leaving home won't help you when someone else pushes the same buttons again. The information will only serve you if you identify the compromise and decide whether you're prepared to make it or not. Either decision will have consequences, but knowing what they are helps you to confront them now. Each time you do this you'll learn something more about yourself.

To respond appropriately to the cry of your emotional alarm, familiarise yourself with the glossary of emotional meanings. As you work through it you'll see that the meanings give general information. To work effectively with this dictionary you'll need to move to the specific by identifying how each message applies to your particular circumstances. In the beginning look up each of your emotions. Soon you'll memorise the list and learn to master your feelings by:

- ❖ identifying the emotion
- ❖ understanding the inner message
- ❖ responding with your decision/s
- ❖ taking action.

This is what's meant by self-control, and once it becomes a new emotional habit you'll easily be able to keep yourself happy most of the time. But when you start working with your emotions this way don't aim for perfection. Instead of using your old emotional habits to tell yourself 'I'm not OK,' rather say, 'I could've handled that better,' and do so the next time. Accept that you're learning new habits and that anything new takes time and lots of practice. Also remember that all your feelings, regardless of whether you label them good or bad, are vital sources of information. Always take the cue from your emotions and slowly start relying on them for feedback. They'll always let you know what's really going on in your life.

THE EMOTIONAL SAGE

You can trust your emotions because they never lie. Many people argue this point because they confuse thoughts with feelings. They tell me that they only do stuff because they feel that they should. Whenever you hear the words 'should', 'ought to' or 'must' realise that you're dealing with your intellect or rational mind. It's a head-trip hiding the fact that you don't really want to.

Test whether it's your head or heart talking by checking whether you feel comfortable with your choices or not. If you hear noisy chatter in your head it's your rational mind playing tricks on you. It can justify any behaviour or decision, become defensive to your detriment and deceive you if need be. Still, no matter what your head tells you, your emotions will seldom be persuaded. You'll continue to feel uncomfortable until you address the underlying problem.

For an example of this think back to the last time you bought a luxury item you knew you couldn't afford. What was your head telling you? Probably after much persuasion it convinced you that your very survival depended upon this desirable item. But how did you feel after you'd bought it?

Although our feelings are so important, we live in a world that dismisses the vital role that they play. This became very apparent when a delegate who runs a computer consultancy confronted me in a seminar. At each mention of the words 'feeling' or 'emotion' he winced visibly. Eventually he couldn't take it anymore and said, 'All this feeling business is just immaturity and weakness. Surely as adults we've moved beyond this and can operate on a higher, more rational level.' I pointed out that if we were pretending that our emotions don't exist, then we were aspiring to be no more than thinking super-computers that are highly sophisticated, but bland. But if we engage our rational thoughts to make sense of our feelings, then he is partially correct. We can never rely purely on the rational to run our lives.

EMOTIONAL TRAFFIC

It takes will to keep our emotions under control and this is a lot simpler than it sounds. All that we need to do is to get into the habit of asking regularly, 'How am I feeling?' If you're happy, know that the choices you're making are right for you. If not, discipline yourself to read the message, understand the meaning and use your rational mind to consider the options. Do you need to make any decisions to redirect your attitude, relationships, career or life?

Regularly asking 'How am I feeling?' is as simple as having an internal traffic light where the red light forces us to stop and listen, the amber to reflect and the green to act on our decisions.

| Stop and listen | Reflect/decide | Take action |

However, if instead of listening to your feelings you run the red light, you'll leave yourself at the mercy of other people. Whether they are parents, spouses, bosses, friends, gurus or even the government, you can always find willing advisors to tell you how to behave. But this feedback comes from their own feelings; it has nothing to do with you.

THE MASK

Buying into this 'people-pleasing' trap means that social niceties will override your own emotions. It's risky, particularly when being polite and proper are at odds with what you're really feeling. As a pattern of a lifetime it's dangerous, because eventually you become a mask and this façade separates you from the substance of your soul. Instead of tapping your own power, fickle social demands will run your life; and until the mask is broken you'll have great difficulty accessing any real feelings.

If we want honest, reliable data, we need to switch off other people's chatter and fine-tune our ability to hear the internal messages. Of course feedback from others can be helpful, but how we feel about it is more useful than taking their comments at face value. Our emotional reaction will tell us whether the information is valuable; and there's a quick test we can run. If we feel angry, hurt, shame or any of the fear-based emotions then these are our feelings and we must deal with them. The person to whom we are responding with this emotion is simply a catalyst to release feelings that we already had. Once these feelings are exposed we need to read the message, address our internal issues, make choices and move on. If, on the other hand, we feel no emotion at all then the message is clear; the comment was more about their needs than our own. So we can ignore it.

APPROPRIATELY INTELLIGENT

In much of this chapter I've referred to dealing with feelings appropriately. This is important because 'appropriateness' is the mark of an emotionally intelligent person. It's what will get you your own way in most situations. Children often behave inappropriately because they haven't yet learnt self-control. They act out their feelings without understanding the consequences. But if we throw our toys around to get our own way in a meeting, we'll be put out on the pavement rather than to bed with no pudding.

So how we manage the power of our feelings is an important criterion for success. If we use our will-power to deal with them internally, we need never lay them on other people. This immediately eliminates accusations like, 'You make me feel ...'. As we've seen, blame drains our personal power and puts people's backs up rather than gaining their co-operation. But going the route 'I feel ... and, therefore, I must deal with it' avoids carrying damaging emotional baggage into our relationships. It clears the path for more open communication.

Being appropriate also means that there's no right or wrong way of dealing with things. It's a matter of doing whatever it takes to make things happen your way. Yes, this sounds manipulative – possibly even cynical – but successful people get away with it because they manoeuvre situations so that everybody wins. They can do this because they've learnt to master their most powerful resource: the intelligence of their emotions. You can too and you'll notice that when you stop letting your feelings hang out you'll start retrieving your power. The more you do so, the deeper the sense of happiness you'll find. This will liberate your creative life-force which is one hundred per cent necessary for you to exploit your full potential. It's what being emotionally intelligent is all about.

Danger –
highly reactive

Now that we know how important our emotions are, it becomes obvious that we can't change our feelings but we can alter how we respond to them. It's what a healthy level of EQ boils down to. This is put into perspective when we consider that if we lived in solitude on a desert island, it wouldn't matter whether we dealt with our feelings or not. If we lost our temper, laughed like a manic hyena, burst into a flood of tears or went into a frenzied rage, the fauna and flora probably wouldn't bat an eyelid, or even shed a little leaf for that matter. Making a noise would only attract attention; and while it could mean that we get eaten, life itself would carry on.

Allowing our feelings to create a commotion when we're with other people is likely to have much the same effect. Acting out just makes a racket. It attracts attention, but usually the wrong kind. People avoid us, ridicule or ignore our behaviour – we end up not getting what we want. So it's the way that we react to others as well as to our feelings that makes all the difference. These two factors are key elements in emotional fitness. They are the reason that EQ is critical if we hope to access our power and do more than merely survive.

Even if you consider yourself to be highly independent or a loner, there are always times when you have to relate to and rely on other people. We often think of artists and sculptors as self-sufficient, but you'd be surprised at how much they depend on the support and co-operation of others.

At an exhibition of women's work that I attended, an artist quickly shattered my opinion of the romantic life of a painter. 'The only time that I can paint is at night,' she said. 'My days are so busy with other things. I'm calling agents, dealing with galleries – marketing myself, I suppose. I'm working on accounts, talking to my bookkeeper, really doing much the same as anyone else who's self-employed.' So much for being driven purely by inspiration and a gooey colourful palette!

REACTIONS COUNT

Whether you're a CEO, a job boss on a building site, a secretary or a home-maker, the way that you react to others will determine how successful you'll be. This is controlled directly by how we deal with our feelings. If, instead of reading the messages, we inflict our crabby moods on others, we're likely to get zero co-operation. We know this whenever we've yelled at the kids to hoover the carpet or whined at our spouse to take out the garbage.

For our artist the same applies. To get her work onto walls anywhere, she needs to do much more than impress gallery owners with the quality of her paintings. And it doesn't matter how brilliant they may be! For us it's no different. In reality we're all in the business of selling ourselves and making things happen depends on our response to other people.

In Africa this is one of the key notions governing traditional life. Generations have been raised on a central cultural script known locally as *ubuntu*. It translates into a deep-rooted knowledge of the fact that both my survival and success are due to the love, help, support and understanding of other people. The reality is the same for Western cultures. The difference is that we've forgotten how important it is. Sometimes its significance is even pooh-poohed. During the annual Academy Awards, when the best directors, actors and song writers thank their producers, mothers, lovers, or pet dog for their support, do we believe them? For many of us the superficiality of the occasion is as far as the realisation goes.

No one can go it alone

Yet none of us could've arrived at where we are today without the care, friendship, encouragement, tolerance, backing, guidance, thoughtfulness, inspiration, nurturing and even financial help of others. Think how this applies to your own history. The number of people who've in some way made an impact on your life probably amounts to hundreds of forgotten souls. It could've been a major contribution like a great opportunity or even something as easily given as an encouraging smile. Then consider why they did it for you. The answer is obvious. They did it because they liked you; they liked the way that you responded to them. It made them feel good. Otherwise they wouldn't have lifted a finger.

Cultivate co-operation

Whenever I conduct seminars in business I urge delegates to think about all the people currently involved in their success. No matter whether these are senior executives or salespeople, most of them initially come up with a very short list. But once we start working through it they quickly understand that even the person who orders the tea or answers the phone participates in the process. Then I ask them to consider how they treat each of these individuals.

Because this is what makes the difference between a smooth path or an obstacle course of frustration. So regardless of whether you like the person or not, make sure that you're doing everything possible to cultivate all of these important relationships. After all, anyone can choose whether they're going to support or sabotage your achievements.

Now this doesn't mean that to get co-operation we always have to be 'nice'. Being 'nice' is as transparent as plastic food wrap and others quickly see through our manipulations. Rather it's about being real. If we work with our own emotional messages instead of letting our feelings run riot, we're sure to be more appropriate in our reactions.

Often when people first learn this they think it means that we're not supposed to talk about our feelings. It doesn't. If we've dealt with our own emotional 'stuff' first, it makes the issue we're struggling with far more palatable for others to hear. The mechanics of this will be fully explored in a later chapter. But for the moment what we need to understand is that to reach this level of emotional maturity we have to re-learn some of our deeply ingrained emotional reactions.

HOME BASE

Our emotional lives had their foundations laid at our parents' knees. Children learn mostly by imitation; and instead of being taught how to deal with our feelings we picked up our parents' habits. Like us, they learnt from their parents, so how we react now probably mimics the practices of many generations in our past. It will combine all our parents' growth and learning as well as their bad habits.

The powerful influence that they had on us will also have determined what we believe to be our 'normal' state of mind. The baseline diagram on page 47 shows how this works. Emotionally we have two extremes – anxiety and stress on the one hand and depression and inertia on the other. Before you or any of your siblings were born, your parents would have established an emotional climate in the home. Even if they were divorced or a single-parent raised you, over the years a recognisable pattern will have developed. This could have been at either one of the two extremes or at any point along the vertical line.

This is relevant because wherever your home climate was on the graph is what you'll consider to be 'normal' now. It's your emotional baseline, the state of mind from which you function. If you were lucky you were raised at the midpoint with happiness as a normal baseline state.

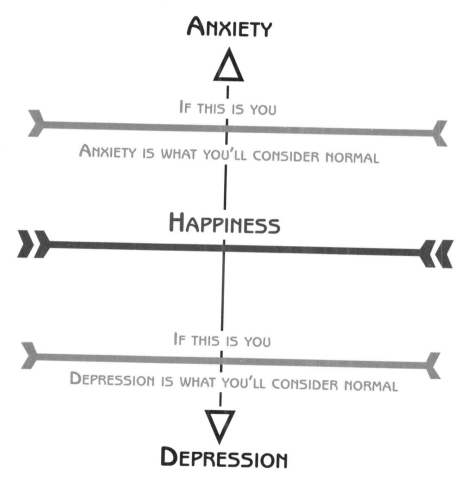

However, recent research in the US shows that with each new generation levels of EQ are declining. This is concerning because it suggests that many young people are creating our tomorrows from emotional foundations closer to one of the unhappy extremes. It doesn't bode well for peace and prosperity in future.

If you accept anything but happiness as your baseline, either a degree of anxiety or misery will be running your life-script. Neither is a cheerful place to live. Both are just comfort zones: known points to which we return habitually. We're lured back to them, not because they're comfortable or they work for us, but only because they're familiar. But we're mistaken if we consider an unhappy baseline a safe place to be. It makes us insecure because it means our emotional lives were built on a foundation of limiting beliefs. These are false self-perceptions that convince us to believe 'This is the way I am. I can't change.' And we stay stuck there. It's why switching jobs or moving town has little impact on breaking our unhappy patterns. Neither is enough to release us from the life-script determining how we use our power.

FEELING LOW?

Each of the extreme points has behaviours and reactions that are typically identified as follows. Depression is about poor management of power; and if your home life was closer to this line, you'll find motivating yourself difficult. You'll be likely to wait for things to happen rather than taking the bull by the horns yourself.

In severe cases your actions will almost apologise for your existence and you'll tend to conform rather than stand out from the crowd. From your parents' patterns you may also have picked up blaming others as a best defence and could find it difficult to take responsibility for your actions now. You'll probably also wallow in the negative side of life. All these are learnt emotional habits. They are not normal conditions for you.

FEELING STRESSED?

On the other hand, people raised closer to the extreme of high anxiety often confuse anxiety with motivation. They can't get going until the pressure is on. Living on their nerves, they're worn out by their own anxiety and are exhausted most of the time. Unable to trust anybody, they think their own security comes from controlling others and they override other people's creative input in the process. Dominating others also consumes their will-power so there's little left for self-control. Usually these people are prone to emotional outbursts and their personal lives are in disarray. If you fall into this category, it's anything but normal. Remember, 'normal' is about happiness, the place where you feel relaxed and content. It's the balance in the middle: the emotional space where you're comfortable with your own power.

Some people may identify with behaviours in both groups. This happens in families where one or both parents lived with an anxious depression. People in this category fall back on the depression/inertia baseline, but use their anxiety and stress to motivate themselves. In the low-energy baseline state, their worry creates sufficient stress to kick their butt into action. People here are often great starters, but seldom finish what they begin. Because of the high levels of anxiety, they lack staying power, burn out quickly and lose interest.

LAYING THE GROUNDWORK

Any of these reactions will occur in different degrees depending on how close your family was to the emotional extremes. But if you recognise parts of yourself in any one of these scenarios, it's possible to change your baseline if you choose. It'll take being constantly aware of your feelings and understanding that gloom on the one hand or anxiety and stress on the other have nothing to do with who you fundamentally are. They are learnt behaviours. As such they can be changed.

To start shifting your baseline, stop accepting depression or anxiety as your normal state and begin working with the messages communicated by your feelings. Remember that your feelings will always tell you when your happiness is threatened. If you've ignored them in the past, they'll probably be screaming at you now. This will manifest as either high anxiety or a deep depression.

It doesn't matter how long these feelings have gone on for, they will be crying out for you to change something in your life. When working to move your baseline bear in mind that you're dealing with a life-long emotional routine. So be patient with yourself. Anyone who's quit a lengthy bad habit will tell you that it's not easy. It takes constant will-power at first, but gets better all the time. After much practice new, healthier habits will eventually replace the old unhappy patterns.

THE FOUNDATION OF POWER

If we don't change the emotional baseline that we adopted as a child it will leave a deep imprint on us for the rest of our lives. This is relevant because our baseline determines how we use our power.

It affects our actions and dictates how we respond, particularly in our relationships. To illustrate this, think about how you behaved as a child when you didn't get the special toy that you wanted. Did you stamp your feet or did you sulk? Now when you don't get a promotion or even your own way, are you tempted to lose your temper or keep your mouth shut and withdraw? Whatever your response is now, it's probably similar to your childlike reaction.

Our early emotional learning is so deeply rooted in us because these patterns are more or less formed before we're ten years old. By the time that we are adults they've become habits we're seldom consciously aware of. If something happens, we react. To explain this we need to go back a bit in time. As early human beings our emotions were part of our survival kit. If we felt frightened, the feeling would instantly send a message to our body to act. This is why when we feel fear, blood – saturated with adrenalin – rushes to our large muscles. It gives us the strength to run or fight. It's not a voluntary action, it just happens.

As emotions are the power behind our survival, it makes sense that they need to be fully developed at a young age. It's no different from a new-born animal learning to walk within the first hour. If, like humans, it took a couple of years to get mobile, the species would have been wiped out long ago. For us, not being able to respond to our feelings would've had the same effect.

In two brains

This thinking led researchers to conclude that we have two separate and distinct parts of our brain – one dealing specifically with emotions, the other with rational thinking. To ensure our survival the emotional brain develops quickly and it's completely formed by the age of eight. Our rational mind – not that essential to our existence – takes longer and is only fully functional by late teens. This is why we're so impressionable when we're young. We absorb everything because we don't yet have the rational equipment to discern whether others' opinions of us are true or false. If we're emotionally immature adults, it can also mean that we're still reacting to situations from an eight-year-old's perspective.

Tom, a vice-president in an accounting practice, spent a long time complaining to me about his staff. 'They're worse than my kids,' he snapped. 'They squabble about nothing, need spoon-feeding and never stop whining! I have to kiss-ass to get anything done. Then there's a long face. I've had it! They're all highly educated people but I get more out of my four- and six-year-olds than I do from this lot!' Tom felt strongly that business should be an objective, rational process. But no matter how much we may like to believe this, in any relationship – business or otherwise – we keep running up against other people's emotions.

THE NERVE CENTRE

The problem Tom was facing happens because our rational mind has its beginnings in the emotional brain. To explain this we need to examine briefly how our brain evolves and here the growth of the world's major cities is a good analogy. In the early life of every major centre, pioneers haphazardly built houses, stores and a few roads and railway tracks to service their immediate needs. Progress meant that the town started to sprawl and the new infrastructure kept extending further and further from its core. Today many cities still have these original routes connected to the CBD. They are the bane of town planners' lives because they determine the way that the city functions and restrict modern development. We can apply this analogy to the emotional and rational brain.

The original CBD can be likened to the emotional brain and the main arterial routes start the growth in the suburbs – or rational mind. So for Tom, no matter how much book learning his staff had done, they were only developing new roads in the suburbs – new pathways in the rational mind. Even if their college degrees had built many new intellectual pathways, these wouldn't have impacted on their behaviour. This is so because our reactions are dictated by the central core: the emotional brain. All the suburban paths in the rational mind have little influence on the core except to put pressure on it. So books may entertain our rational mind, but we only mature our EQ when we grow from our experiences.

It's no wonder that Tom was so frustrated because not even our education system understands this. Like his staff we got through the drill of formal education but were essentially unprepared for life in the real world. The three Rs and history, geography, philosophy, maths and science may have developed our rational mind, but we emerged from school still lacking life-experience.

In fact our education taught us to be so dependent on our intellect that many people now dismiss their feelings and live exclusively in their heads. They've studied the right books and can even quote from all the literature. But unless they apply the learning to their lives, this amounts to little more than intellectual masturbation.

RUNNING WILD

Even if we see ourselves as highly rational people, our emotional brain still dominates our lives. It's bound up with our survival and if we're threatened our emotions take full control. Picture yourself walking in the bush when suddenly you're charged by a fierce animal. Would you stand there thinking, 'Well – maybe I can fight it off ... ummm ... it looks quite big – perhaps I'd better run and run now'? No! In a split second the emotional brain switches into gear and before we know it we've already reacted.

In our hi-tech world wild beasts are not our concern, but the same thing happens when someone pushes us too far. If we need to respond quickly our feelings instantly unplug the rational mind and we're left at the mercy of our emotional brain. Whenever we lose our temper or are frozen with fear or overwhelmed with grief, our rational mind literally goes completely off-line.

Our rational mind is the will keeping our emotions under control, so when it's uncoupled we experience a colossal surge of explosive power. Daniel Goleman calls this an 'emotional hijacking'; and while it's happening we're held hostage to the demands of the emotional brain. It plunges us into the depths of our feelings and for that moment we often start responding from the perspective we had when we were eight years old. If we were angry then, we'll be destructive now. Road-rage is a good example of just how crazed some people can become.

Sometimes emotional hijackings can be so severe that afterwards we don't recall what happened. Lorena Bobbit claimed this after lopping off her husband's penis – it's possible that a hijacking made her temporarily insane. Extreme cases of distress can unhinge any of us. Normal, balanced people who've had a major car accident will tell you this. At the time they may have been conscious but were so shocked that they couldn't remember what happened.

Even if we're not running riot on the roads or 'Bobbiting' our husbands, angry emotional hijackings are dangerous. When our rage unplugs our rational mind, our mouths connect directly to our emotional brain and we frequently say horrible things that we may not mean. This is destructive because it severely damages our relationships. Think about some of the things that you said the last time you were angry. Can you 'un-say' them now that you're calmer?

In TV courtroom dramas it always amuses me when the judge instructs the jury to disregard remarks that witnesses have made. How can anyone ignore comments that have already influenced their opinion? In our relationships this means that apologies seldom erase the hurtful things we've said. The wound has been inflicted; the damage is already done. Even if the other person is forgiving, his or her view of us or the degree to which he or she will trust us in future is changed forever.

WARNING!

We can avoid destructive hijackings by using our bodies as a valuable resource. Remember that our physical, emotional, mental and spiritual components operate as a system. So just before losing it emotionally, we all experience a physical symptom. This serves as a warning signal – a loud siren to tell us what's going on. Seminar delegates that I've worked with generally report these symptoms to be one or more of the following sensations: trembling in the hands, face or lips; a burning heat in the ears; a flushed or drained feeling in the face; heart pounding in the chest; a very quiet or very loud voice; a fluttering in the stomach; tightness around the neck; clenching of fists or tearfulness.

To identify your warning symptom, think back to the last time that you lost your temper. What happened to you physically moments before you exploded? It may be one of the symptoms mentioned above or something quite different. Whatever it is, it's important to recognise your own warning signal and remember it. The next time you feel this sensation use it as a reminder to keep your rational brain on-line – even if it means counting to ten! This takes will-power and you can develop it by practising this technique over and over again.

Most angry hijackings occur because of the baggage in our emotional brain. The 'stuff' we've collected along the way makes us respond inappropriately at times. Our memory hangs onto emotionally charged experiences and in particular to the sad and painful ones that cause us most harm. Usually these strong attachments to our past resurface as hijackings in our adult lives. They're already charged with emotion and it doesn't take much to trigger an explosion.

REGURGITATING EVENTS

Although it's possible to remember every event in our lives we seldom chew the cud over mundane incidents. To illustrate this, pick any date in the past – let's say 30 August 1997. Can you recall what you were doing? Unless it was your birthday or another special event, you probably won't remember. Then cast your mind back to 31 August of the same year – the day you heard that Princess Diana had died. Even if you're not an avid royal supporter it's likely that you'll recollect what you were up to when the tragic news broke.

It's never the actual event that imprints itself into our memory but more our interpretation thereof. This translates into the amount of energy invested in our reaction to it. In itself no experience is good or bad. These judgements are interpretations we've made depending upon whether we gained or lost power. Have you ever listened to brothers and sisters talking about their early home lives? Sometimes it sounds like the voices of three or four separate families. Even if we lived in the same household or went to the same school, our experiences will be decoded differently and our interpretation is what we'll remember. This is what makes us act out inappropriately at times.

Good memories make us feel better, but bad times remembered drag us down. Like an emotional time-capsule, recollections thrust us back into the feeling and it's as convincing as if we were right there all over again. Of course we don't mind remembering exciting times; but what do we do with the negative garbage in our mind? Anything can trigger such a memory and we can't hide from the damaging effect it has on us now.

SORTING THE ARCHIVES

To address this think of your memory as two filing cabinets storing your life experiences; one you've labelled positive, the other negative and bad. All experiences, whether we think of them as good or not, hold the power to teach us something significant about ourselves. Events in the negative archives are only filed there if we haven't yet learnt everything we can from the experience. Each one traps a degree of power – the energy we need to handle the situation – and this pent-up force plugs our mind into the past event. It's like tagging our finger to remind us to learn from the experience. These memories also hurt because emotional pain is telling us to get the lesson so that we can move on. When we do so – even if it's years later – we release the trapped power and the value of the experience changes. It becomes a positive opportunity for self-discovery and this is how negative burdens can be re-filed as benefits to us.

Again, like reading the message of your feelings, you only need to do this when you're reminded of the bad experience. If something triggers a sensitive memory, stop yourself and think carefully about what you learnt from that particular experience. Even in the darkest corners, where your files are filled with shame and anguish, something valuable can be extracted from the things that happened to you.

I first saw the profound significance of this when, a few years ago, I worked privately with Susie – a mother of two in her mid-thirties. Throughout most of her twelve-year marriage she had stayed at home and for the past ten years her husband James had abused her. For her the physical blows were less damaging than the emotional abuse. She was so resigned to it that she even said, 'You know, the bruises are the easiest to heal.'

As in many cases of abuse, James had convinced her that she was to blame. Susie commented, 'When I'd find out about his affairs he'd sneer at me and say that I was a fat, ugly cow so what did I expect. If I asked him to do anything for the children he'd yell – always yelling – and say that it was my job. Mostly we'd fight and argue about money. It was strange because I knew that he earned plenty; but I had to scrimp and save even to cover the basics for the boys.'

When I started working with Susie she'd taken their sons and left him for the fourth and final time. Looking back on her twelve years she was deeply embarrassed. She kept repeating, 'I'm so ashamed. I was such a fool. Why did I stay? I used to be so strong. I just don't know what happened.' What Susie didn't see was that she was still strong. After many years of verbal, physical and emotional abuse she'd have to be relatively robust to have remained stable for so long. For her the problem wasn't a lack of inner strength but more that she'd invested her power in him.

As we worked through the events of her marriage, she cautiously started taking out some of the old files; and step-by-step she began to perceive that she was much hardier than she thought. Instead of being ashamed, she also came to terms with how courageous she'd been in coping with the vicious attacks. She learnt what she could endure or wouldn't tolerate any longer; and by retrieving her power saw just how much she had to give. 'If there's a next time,' she joked, 'it'll be to the right person!'

Deep into the process, Susie became aware of her own needs – the needs she'd suppressed. She began to understand that because of her emotional dependency she'd unwittingly allowed the abuse to continue. For her it was a difficult time; but the more we went through it, the more she found out who she really was. By the time Susie was ready to move on, she said somewhat hesitantly, 'I hate to admit it, but maybe if it hadn't been for my life with him, I wouldn't now know who I really am.' It's a hell of a way to learn, but after much hard work on herself she came out of it better for the experience.

Susie and I keep in touch; and by getting something profound out of each of those negative files she had the energy to face life as a single parent. Although her 'next time' hasn't happened yet, she now runs her own real estate company that's doing really well. At home her two well-adjusted teenage sons keep her company and she reports having never been happier or more satisfied than she is right now.

EXPERIENCES MAKE YOU UNIQUE

From Susie's ordeal we learn that ignoring our experiences won't turf them out of our mind. All the chapters of her life, even the awful ones, held important information for her. Like her, each episode we resolve makes us interesting; and attempting to ignore bad experiences is like trying to amputate essential parts of ourselves. No one escapes bad times, no matter how privileged they may seem.

Just think of the Kennedys, the Gettys or any other seemingly advantaged family. All have had their share of hardships to cope with. In previous generations enduring misfortune was thought to be character-building. Today it still is, but what makes the difference now is how we deal with it. When we learn and grow from our experiences we see the value in the difficult times we've had. This automatically shifts the records from a negative to a positive file.

GO EASY ON YOURSELF

Now if this tempts you into a sudden spring-cleaning of your emotional brain, don't do it! A major clean-out makes you so busy with mental housework that you'll forget to live in the meanwhile. I've seen many people try to make it all OK now, now, NOW! They go a little loco in the process. Accept that it'll never be. There's years and years of stuff in there. Some of it may need addressing now while other parts can be left alone. Acknowledge that you've coped until this point in your life and allow your memory to guide you in future. When something triggers it you'll get the information that you need. Trust yourself and make this your new habit rather than hoping for an instant fix right now.

Another hint about the baggage in our emotional brain comes from the way we react to our circumstances. You can use your feelings to test yourself here. If you've responded in a way that leaves you feeling uncomfortable, the discomfort is a message to change this particular reaction. Remember that you can't reverse the situation as it has already happened. But you can work on it to make sure that you don't feel uncomfortable again.

You do this by first looking up the message of the emotion. What were you feeling that made you react in this way? Was it anger, frustration, guilt, anxiety or perhaps hurt? Learn from the message. Then picture yourself in the same situation again and visualise reacting differently. This kind of mental rehearsal is powerful because it schools our mind to respond in new ways. While you're training your will-power, bear in mind that it may not work the first time – or even the tenth time. But the more you practise it, the sooner your reaction will change. This method can be used to change any of our responses, including emotional hijackings.

KEEPING HEAD ABOVE WATER

So when it comes to EQ the message is about changing learnt behaviours that no longer serve you. It doesn't mean changing who you fundamentally are. So it's not about chucking the baby out with the bath water only to start again. In any field it's known that a shift can only effectively happen by building on the existing paradigm. Therefore it's important to start with where you're at right now. Be comforted by the fact that everything that you need is already inside you. It's just waiting for you to hear the messages and respond.

Whether it's your baseline or some of your reactions, the things that you learnt originally put you onto the starting blocks of life. How you swim the race is a choice that only you can make. The fact that you've survived until now means that you've already learnt to float. Acknowledge that you're most of the way there. If you find that you're splashing around in the shallow end getting nowhere, it may be that only your swimming strokes or style need some attention.

Unfortunately you can't take a pill to become emotionally mature, but you can choose to change some of your responses. In life this means looking at our behaviour towards other people as well as how we react to our circumstances. Remember that if you're unhappy no one is to blame, not even you. You can forgive yourself because you've never learnt to work with your feelings. Start now and develop new habits and happier patterns that ultimately are more likely to get you what you want. While you're working with this, remember that it's not about self-improvement. It's about being able to maximise the reactions that work for you and minimise the ones that don't. After all, trying to improve who you fundamentally are will only damage your self-esteem and this is the subject of our next chapter.

The buddy system

A while ago a friend of mine was chatting to her seven-year-old son and she asked him who his best friend was. 'You know, Mom,' piped up the little fellow, 'I am. Because I'm the only one who has to live with me for the rest of my life.' Wisdom straight from the mouths of babes, I thought. In just one statement this little boy had encapsulated what the self-esteem movement has been trying to teach us for decades. I hope he hangs onto it forever.

Being our own best friend is the foundation of a healthy EQ, but as adults it's something many people grapple with. Instead we're more likely to put ourselves down or dismiss our efforts with harmful self-criticism. Telling yourself that you're useless, incapable, ugly, fat and horrible doesn't change the things that aren't working in your life. It just makes you crazy. While it's normal to give yourself some grief, unrelenting self-bashing is symptomatic of your mind attacking itself. Beating yourself up only creates an enemy within and this sadistic beast wages a war you can never win. It feeds on your energy, sabotages your efforts and has a paralysing effect on your life. If you think about it, why take on any new challenge if you know that it'll mean hours of self-criticism before you even begin? It will stunt your growth and just make you scared of yourself.

To put this self-created enemy into perspective, think about what would happen if you accused your friends of the awful things that you tell yourself. Imagine saying some of these things to someone else:

'You're such a cretin. Nothing ever works out for you.'

'Phew! Look at all that cellulite. Yuck!'

'You stupid idiot! What do you expect?'

If you did this, it's quite likely that you wouldn't have these friends for long. So why do we persist in treating ourselves this way?

IS BELIEVING IN YOURSELF ARROGANT?

Popular misconceptions cloud the real meaning of self-esteem and it's our faulty thinking that convinces us that self-bashing is OK. One of these inaccuracies is to confuse believing in yourself with vanity. Self-preening goes against the grain of deep-rooted social and religious values like modesty and humility. If you hold these in high regard, the vanity view of self-esteem may appear to be conceited, even evil.

Another fallacy is that a high level of self-esteem leads to arrogant behaviour. Even a dictionary of mine defines self-esteem as 'an excessively favourable opinion of oneself'. It's no wonder that we're all so baffled. But self-esteem has nothing to do with arrogance. They're at opposite ends of two extremes. Arrogant people don't believe in themselves. That is why they're always talking about how important they are. They're not convinced so they're trying to sway you. Insecurity breeds arrogance and vanity; neither has anything to do with healthy self-esteem.

Self-esteem is about believing in who you are. It boils down to no more than accepting yourself warts and all – this is how it works for me. Not by any stretch of the imagination could it be said that I'm a maths genius. But I've learnt that there's no point in letting this – or any of my other so-called weaknesses – affect what I can do well. Likewise, the things that you're not good at needn't interfere with the degree to which you value your abilities, talents, creativity and unique way of doing things.

MIRROR, MIRROR

This is vital because how we feel about ourselves produces the face that we show the world. It's the one that counts most; because whether we're going on a date or for a job interview, our self-esteem decides the outcome. If you think about it, why should others give you any more respect than you give yourself? Or if you don't believe in your own capabilities, how can you convince anyone else to? But real problems arise when others reflect back our miserable self-view. Mostly we take offence. If this happens, ask yourself, 'What am I thinking that's making people treat me this way?' You can be sure it'll be something rooted in your thinking. To change the way that other people relate to you, your most important first step is to make friends with the person in the mirror.

Start by evaluating how you talk to yourself. Every day our mind babbles on telling us thousands of things. Mostly we're not even conscious of it. But – like the ancient people of America – learn to stalk these fleeting thoughts. When you catch them, check each against the following question: 'If my buddies told me this, how would I feel about them?'

Your answer will let you know whether you're creating an internal friend or foe. If your sentiments sound like the enemy's words, reframe your thoughts. Find something positive to say. When something goes wrong, reprimanding yourself with 'You're a bloody fool!' will only make you more frustrated. Why lose energy by putting yourself down when it's just as easy to say something kinder like 'I'm doing the very best I can'?

To give you an idea of your level of self-esteem, you may want to turn to the standard adult self-esteem test in appendix 2. It's a simple pen-and-pencil inventory that will show you how much you value yourself. Once you've completed it bear in mind that self-esteem can fluctuate. If you did the test when you were feeling great, the result will be different from when you're at a low ebb. Whatever your result, it will give you an idea of how much you need to do to start valuing yourself.

SELF-ESTEEM SHOWS

A healthy self-esteem will lead to confidence – not arrogance – which is easy for others to recognise. They read it in the way we carry ourselves, our body language, tone of voice and facial expressions. It's picked up not from what we say but how we say it. Others can assess our self-esteem not only from our physical appearance, but from the way in which we present the full package.

When Nelson Mandela was imprisoned for those long years, his gaolers – who perceived him as public enemy number one – were reported to have said: 'Though we always see him in tatty prison clothes, you can just sense this humble man is a powerful leader.' They had stripped him of all the usual trappings of success. Even so, they perceived the strength of his dignity from the way in which he treated them and his fellow inmates. Cosmetic things such as power dressing, fancy cars and offices won't cover the blemishes in your self-esteem. Whatever you think about yourself will always shine through. Mostly it will be reflected in your achievements.

Successful people have one thing in common – they believe in their own abilities, and it shows. They have respect for themselves as well as for others and tend to have good-quality relationships. These people have a presence and we can sense that they are natural leaders. They're outspoken independent thinkers whose hopeful, positive and optimistic attitude commands co-operation. Unlike arrogant people, those with a healthy self-esteem don't bore us with the details of their own self-involvement. At Mandela's inauguration as South Africa's

President he didn't say, 'After all the years of self-sacrifice, what a victory I've won.' Instead, he attributed the glory to those who'd made great personal sacrifices to get him there.

Our level of self-esteem is interwoven with the emotional baseline discussed in the previous chapter on reactions, and it influences the way we interpret reality. We can either view events in a matter-of-fact way or allow our enemy tenant to take things personally. A call from a friend was a powerful illustration of this. She's recently fallen head-over-heels in love and is feeling on top of the world. Her knight in shining armour is saying and doing all the right things; but if he doesn't call, her self-doubt comes flooding back. This is reflected in the way she talks about the relationship. 'I know he's busy,' she'll say, 'but sometimes I just feel like I don't deserve to be this happy.' Unless she starts to believe in her own value, her knight will have an uphill battle defeating her doubtful dragon. It could potentially destroy the relationship.

DEFEAT THAT DRAGON

Holding onto this voice of self-doubt is unwise. Rather think of it as a passing message telling you to work on your self-esteem. Feelings such as 'I'm not good enough' come from the negative expressions of your childhood. Reverse them by proving the opposite. Confirm that you are worthwhile by remembering specific incidents that prove your value. This technique quietens the childlike wail and helps you to gain a healthier respect for yourself.

Many people have a problem with this and believe that being harsh on themselves is the only means to self-improvement. If they're not lambasting themselves all the time they think they're not learning. If you recognise yourself here, then think about this: the enemy within never improves you – it just keeps you fighting. It puts you on the defensive and inevitably you emerge the worse for wear.

I came across an extreme case of this when I worked with Jack, a business executive. He believed that every success that he had would be followed by an equal degree of punishment. 'When I was eleven,' he said, 'my father abandoned my mother and me for another woman and we never heard from him again. My mother was struggling to get a job, so I helped her when she started a small business. My father was wealthy then and I suppose that I somehow connected his riches to my own pain.' Jack realised that it was illogical to think this way; but as a little boy he'd believed that his father's wealth was the thing that had made leaving his mother possible. In his mind his father's riches had been the biggest threat to him.

'You can imagine,' he observed, 'that this left me with some rather strange contradictions about success. As much as I wanted my mother to succeed, it could've meant that the same thing would happen all over again. We were religious, so to settle my worries I made a pact with God. I told Him that I would take any punishment if my mother's business survived and she stayed with me.'

Whipping boy

Today Jack is a multimillionaire, but his life-long belief in self-punishment means that he's taken many whippings along the way. He's had two uncomfortable marriages and a number of people that he trusted embezzled large amounts from him. He's learnt that being tough on himself meant that he was hard on others; and instead of celebrating his success they deeply resented him. Over the time that we worked together, he saw how his beliefs had affected his decisions. He'd literally set himself up for punishment. Now that he's given up his life-sentence, Jack is beginning to really enjoy what he's created. For the first time he's also starting to see himself as successful.

The enemy always feeds on self-criticism; and the more sustenance you give it, the greater its influence. It keeps your mind focused on your negative points and coerces you into doing the very things you're fighting against. For example being hypercritical about your weight won't make you stick to your diet. Quite likely it'll do the opposite. Likewise, telling yourself that you're ill won't make you healthy and reminding yourself of your failures won't help you to become successful. Instead of fighting, disarm the enemy within. Starve it of power by focusing on your good points. It often helps to set up a dialogue with this sadistic scoundrel. Whenever it tempts you to sabotage your efforts tell it firmly, 'Sod off! I'm going to win today!'

REDRAW THE LANDSCAPE

Although our self-image may now seem as if it's cast in stone, it is in fact only something that we've created. It's a life's work in the making and it started with things that we have been repeatedly told. Our emotional reaction to this early commentary planted the thoughts firmly in our mind and now these words repeat themselves in our heads. We know that they also replay similar feelings. The problem is that the more you repeat them, the more you're likely to believe them, even if they were originally lies.

Goëbbels, the Nazi in charge of propaganda, was reported to have said, 'If you tell a lie often enough people will believe it to be true.' This principle underpinning brainwashing also applies to self-esteem: the negativity that we repeatedly heard when we were young produces the same result. You'll recall from an earlier chapter that these thoughts were absorbed straight into the emotional brain long before our rational mind was sufficiently developed to be discerning enough to discard them.

Imagine that these thoughts charged with bad feelings are pathways in your mind and each time that you say these negative things you make the groove deeper. I'm a keen off-road cyclist and when on a trail it always amazes me how quickly nature restores itself. Although a path may look well worn, if it hasn't been used for a few weeks it quickly becomes overgrown. This got me thinking about the thought pathways in the mind. Put up a 'no-entry' sign on these negative tracks – especially the ones that resurrect old bad feelings – and know that there's no need to go down them again. Programme in more positive pathways instead; and soon the well-trodden harmful-thought trails will become overgrown and eventually disappear.

HEAD OR HEART – WHO WINS?

But be aware that just thinking positive thoughts isn't enough. Emotions carry the power that drives your mind; so if there's a conflict between your head and heart, your emotions will always win. This is why the positive-thinking movement has had limited success. I saw a powerful illustration of this a couple of years ago when a friend of mine was particularly enthusiastic about a positive-thinking programme he'd been on. Every day Jeremy religiously worked the techniques he'd learnt. It didn't take him long – probably about 20 minutes in the morning. Within two months the business he'd been struggling with started to turn around. He was winning contracts he'd only dreamt of; and because things were working out, he grew lazy about his daily techniques. Six months passed and his new-found success dwindled. After a year he was struggling in much the same way as before.

When I asked him why he wasn't using the powerful tools that had worked well for him, he said unenthusiastically, 'I don't know, I suppose I really must get back to doing my mental exercises.' We've talked since and Jeremy knows that the problem is his low self-esteem. When he was using the techniques he was boosting himself daily; but as soon as he stopped, his heavy heart swamped any positive thinking. Now he's working with his emotions; and instead of feeling that he doesn't deserve to be successful, he's starting to value his own resources. 'It's amazing,' he said, 'it's so much easier, because when I feel good, thinking positively no longer means battling against my old negative emotional self.'

Positive thinking is very good for you, but it's not enough. If you're not doing anything about what's making you feel down, your positive thoughts will be like covering a cow-pie in whipped cream and topping it with a few cherries to pretty things up! The result may look better, but the proof of the pudding is definitely in the eating. To enjoy the cake as well as the frosting, we need to master both our thoughts and our feelings. Thoughts and feelings run your mind, which in turn governs your life. Both are the building blocks that create your existence because they influence every decision that you make. Who you think you are today expresses past choices that you've made and by changing these choices you can dramatically alter your self-image. This will definitely change the course of your life.

TEST YOURSELF

Do this exercise to review your thinking. Divide a piece of paper into three columns. In the first column write down ten things that you think about yourself. In the second and third columns write down ten things that your friends and family think about you respectively. Don't read any further until you've done this on paper.

Now let's examine the lists that you've made. The second and third columns are a list of thoughts that you have imagined reflect the way in which others perceive you. These are actually projections revealing the way that you see yourself. They're important to include because these thoughts are probably a little kinder than those that you have about yourself. While examining your lists question why you've made these choices. These choices are about who you think you are. Consider each thought. What does it make you feel about yourself?

Now put a plus or minus sign against each perception depending on whether it's positive or negative. Add up the pluses and minuses in each column. Which is the higher score? Does this tie up with your self-esteem score from the test in appendix 2? Then cross out the negative thoughts in all three columns. Where does this leave you? Do you believe that it gives you an unreal picture of yourself? If you do, look at these negatives and evaluate what they've done for you in the past. Have they made you feel better? Are they motivating? Have they improved you? Think deeply about this because in all likelihood they've done nothing for you. They're just bullets that the enemy keeps firing at your self-esteem.

Now look at the remaining positive thoughts. Imagine filling your head with these ideas and wiping the negatives clean out of your mind. If you're grappling with this affirmative self-view, it's also possible that you'll find the thought of liking yourself distasteful. Are you concerned that you may fall into the arrogance trap? Remember that believing in yourself is having faith in your abilities. It's different from the insecurity of arrogance. Instead, think of yourself in the same way that you feel about a friend. We aren't passionately in love with our friends. We just like them a lot. The same applies to you. Be as gentle, kind and tolerant with yourself as you are towards your companions and your self-esteem will flourish.

WIDEN YOUR SELF-VIEW

Wisdom begins with having an appropriate picture of yourself. Please note that I did not say 'realistic' because no one can tell you what that means. Many people who believe that they are being 'realistic' are often just confusing realism with the limitations that they've imposed on themselves.

I know a very talented musician who dreamt of becoming a concert pianist. Today she believes that this was an idealistic aspiration and that the most she could have hoped for was a piano stool in a cocktail bar. Who squashed her desires? And why didn't she value herself enough to fight for her dreams?

Like her, many people only live up to the limited ideas that others have of them, and then wonder why happiness and success elude them.

Having an appropriate picture of yourself means understanding who you've been in the past and knowing how to use the present to create who you want to become in the future. You do so by employing your feelings to question your self-image. If this makes you uncomfortable, you are getting a clear message that you need to challenge your thinking. The thoughts that you will need to address are not the fleeting ones, but rather those that are charged with negative emotion. You'll recognise them easily: they are the repetitive thoughts that have the ability to sink you.

TAKE CONTROL

Keep defying your harmful thinking by harnessing the power of your mind. Remember that your mind contains all the resources that you will ever need, but that these are only activated by the energy of love-based, positive emotions. So first use the techniques discussed in the previous chapter to gain control over your feelings and then exercise your will-power to master your thinking. There are two techniques that you can use to take charge of your thoughts: the first is positive affirmations, the second visualisation.

Repeating positive affirmations makes new constructive thoughts firm in your mind and these hatch a healthier adult voice in your head. Unlike the lies that you have believed in the past, they imprint a more favourable impression, which will eventually become part of you. As the well-known Mind Power trainer John Kehoe says, 'The beauty of affirmations is that you don't even have to believe them.' Quite likely you won't. Remember that it's the repetition that holds the power to planting the new idea, not the thought itself. Therefore the louder you can make this adult voice, the deeper the healthy message sinks in.

Affirmations work because positive thoughts excite us; and when we combine this with feeling good our thoughts continually spark the power of our emotions. It doesn't matter whether you say them quietly to yourself or aloud; either way they will have a profound effect on your life. They're easy to use, but don't be deceived by their simplicity. Affirmations are simple but powerful. You can use them to change your belief about being a lousy parent, manager, lover or spouse, or to enhance any aspect of your life. If you want to do better at something, use positive affirmations to reinforce that you can. If you're putting yourself down, change the negative thought into a positive thought and make this your affirmation. In the beginning it will take lots of will-power to drown out the noise of the negative thoughts – but be confident that this harsh voice can be defeated.

Bear in mind that there are a few rules to formulating your affirmations. Affirmations need to be positive, in the present tense (accept it's already happening), personal and to the point. You will stick to all of these rules if you begin each affirmation with 'I am ...'.

'I am healthy, wealthy and successful.'

'I am a great human being.'

'I am in love with life.'

'I am generous, loving and kind.'

'I am energetic.'

'I am special, gifted and talented.'

'I am creative.'

'I am sexy and desirable.'

The great thing about repeating affirmations is that you don't have to make time to work with them. You can say them in traffic, in queues, while waiting on the phone, fetching kids, in the supermarket, in the bath or while cooking a meal. But only choose two or three statements that you're going to work with at one time. I've known people to list 10, 20 and sometimes even 30 statements that they want to repeat to themselves every day. You simply cannot work on so many things at once. Attempting to do so will water down your efforts because you won't get the full value of the repetition. If you're a little unsure of where to start, begin with the list of thoughts that you wrote down about yourself. Either pick the positive thoughts or turn some negative thoughts into the opposite positive and use these as your affirmations.

MAKE MIND MOVIES

The second tool that you can use to tap the power of the mind is 'visualisation' or 'mental rehearsal', as it's sometimes known. Pictures have the most profound effect on our subconscious mind; and when we see ourselves acting or reacting differently we can start reprogramming our lives. Visualisation is like making a movie in your mind. It is an easy technique to master. As the director and main actor you have full control over the script and plot of the film. Take time to do this. Sit comfortably, close your eyes and picture the scenes that you want. How does it feel to see yourself in exactly the situations you desire? Be aware of these feelings because emotions provide the energy to manifest these pictures into reality. Again repetition is the key. You will need to do this every day for quite a few weeks before you see its magical results.

Like affirmations, you can use mental rehearsal to alter any aspect of your life. Many people visualise prosperity and success while others I know have had great success imagining themselves becoming more relaxed or more motivated. Sports stars all over the world know the power of this tool in improving athletic performance. Visualisation has even increased libido with terrific results. You can use it to befriend yourself, tap self-confidence or generate that increase you've been after. Whatever you want, you can be certain that mental rehearsal will help you to get it. For more information on these techniques, one of the most accessible works around is Kehoe's *Mind Power for the 21st Century*.

FREE YOURSELF FROM THE PRISON OF PAIN

If you want to change your life, you need to act every day to maximise the thoughts and feelings that work for you and eliminate those that don't. Yes, it takes will-power in the beginning, but with practice it'll eventually become your new habit – a new way of being. Keep motivated by focusing on the advantages of living the life you want and the benefits will far outweigh the toil. Instead of giving in to your limitations, start working towards your countless possibilities by valuing yourself. Anyone can do it, especially you.

If you've tried the other route of allowing the enemy to behave like a sadistic prison warder, assess how well it's been working. If there's room for improvement then give yourself a chance to be your own best friend. Treat yourself kindly, eliminate those harsh words and you'll see just how much this helps to make the magic happen. Remember that a healthy self-image is simply about being the very best that you can be. So you can stop shopping around for alternative selves because everything that you need is already inside of you. Find it by valuing who you are and lead yourself into your future with you – as your best friend – standing supportively by your side.

Exorcising
your demons

Negativity is deadly for our self-esteem. It drains our life-force and, like a toxin, poisons our beliefs making us feel helpless and apathetic. If we're fresh out of the energy needed to drive our lives, we feel stuck and unable to explore our individuality. Negativity curtails our personal freedom because under its sinister influence we give up control. This binds us to the devil of dependency. So, if you want to be in the driving seat of your life, submitting to negativity is an emotionally unintelligent thing to do.

People with a healthy level of EQ resist negative influences. They don't carp about how bad things are but look for opportunities to make good instead. They use their will-power to control their minds and are optimistic about life, particularly their own. When it comes to bad news emotionally robust people are discerning. They may be well informed, but don't give credence to pessimism by indulging it. These individuals understand the desperate pitfalls of negativity and choose to have no truck with it. Nor should you.

Negativity is all around us. It creeps into our conversations, business deals, friendships – even our faith. And it'll continue for as long as we remain ignorant of its debilitating effect. For me negativity is the source of all evil because under its influence we behave badly, often harming other people. For instance people who are fresh out of personal power are like energy vampires – they suck the power right out of you. Victims, cynics and pessimists do this because they're determined to make everyone else miserable too. They're just unpleasant to be around.

One of the best reasons I heard for not entertaining negativity was given to me by a Kenyan colleague with whom I work. She said, 'When people come into my office with their gripes and moans it feels as if they're opening their mouths to spew their acrid vomit all over me!' Now this may be disgusting but it's definitely true. So if you wouldn't tolerate this physically why become a mental barf-bag for other people's whining? Always think of negativity as vile bile and it'll be a lot easier to put a stop to this unhealthy indulgence.

FEAR PARALYSIS

One of the biggest problems with negativity is that it plays out through our emotional lives. It's dangerous because it's rooted in fear and fear immobilises us. I'll explain the consequences of negativity by using an illustration known as the 'pike syndrome'. This is a well-known experiment conducted with a fish called a pike.

This fish is placed in a tank with a piece of glass separating it from its food. After numerous attempts to get food the pike tires of bumping its nose and eventually gives up. Even when the glass is removed it won't move from its hungry corner. This is exactly how fear operates in our lives.

We can see through our fear, but it immobilises us. It freezes our ability to act. When we're scared we also relinquish control and become puppets to those in authority pulling the strings. Even in the most liberated of countries this happens all the time. We lose our individuality to companies because we're afraid of losing our jobs. We toe the government line if we're scared of the punishment this organisation metes out. Our gurus threaten us with hellfire and brimstone so we place our faith in them. If democracy is supposed to promote freedom, our diet of fear is slowly whittling it away. In real terms individuality cannot exist while we're succumbing to negativity.

Fear produces a fight-or-flight reaction. But when we're faced with horrors like poverty, warfare, incarceration or death we can do neither. So we surrender our power and give in. This makes us dependent and easy to control. Handing over the reins imprisons our soul and plunges us into the dungeons of apathy. Apathetic masses are pessimistic, hopeless and depressed. They follow rather than lead and their minds are vulnerable. Political power-seekers use this. For example, we know that Hitler took advantage of similar conditions to gain power in pre-war Germany. A disheartened society is always susceptible to the promises of those in control; and if we continue to lap up negativity we'll land in a similar boat.

THE HUNGRY MIND

Our mind is the creative force that moves us forward and it craves stimulation. Any stimulation – positive or negative – will do. So if you aren't feeding your mind positively, it'll forage on the environment around you. Daily the tabloids, television or the movies spew out an avalanche of negativity that's suffocating our soul. We keep blaming them when in fact it's our own fears that are making this possible.

In life 'like-finds-like' and the pessimistic outlook we're fed fits comfortably with our own negative views. It confirms how powerless we are and coincides with what we're already feeling. It's so overwhelming that we've stopped questioning whether what we see, hear and read is even true.

Yet if we take the trouble to look we see acts of kindness daily, tender expressions of the incredible spirit within. Human nature is essentially about creativity not destruction, about happiness not depression. But these things don't make news.

Perhaps because we've lost our appetite for them. We keep pointing a finger at the media; but the moment that we stop indulging in our own negative thinking good news will become a viable option. It'll be a significant sign that *en masse* we're starting to retrieve our power.

Our penchant for negativity has nothing to do with who we fundamentally are. It's about how we've been conditioned. But when I suggest that seminar delegates stop supporting media that thrives on negative views, I often experience a defensive outcry. People are concerned that without their daily negative fix they'll develop unbalanced views. But where's the balance in the media? Lots of people I know have stopped reading negative newspapers altogether; they also switch off the news. They find that they're not missing anything. Without a regular dose of murder and mayhem their ability to maintain a cheerful outlook quickly improves.

MASS MIND-CONTROL

Technology has made it possible for news to travel fast; and the reality is that the same negative stories are repeated time and again. If this sounds familiar it's meant to. Remember that just repeating a thought makes us believe it to be true. Whether it's the Middle East, Russia or Rwanda, every day we're programmed with the same diet of human deprivation and cruelty. What has this done to our faith in humanity?

At the pulpit preachers tell us that the cruelty we see is evidence of our propensity for evil. This scares us even more because it supports the view that human beings are essentially rotten creatures. I don't believe this, but it is a powerful way to make us dig into our pockets to pay for our salvation. More plausibly, brutality points to how fear is acted out in our society – and we're addicted to it. We're exposed to so few positive role models that I've even heard characters like Jeffrey Dahmer being used as a benchmark. Some people think that even though they have cut a few personalities down to size, at least they didn't have them for lunch!

Media technology has become our modern form of human consciousness. It colonises our mind with fear; and unless we're discerning, someone else controls our thinking every day. If you think that we're not being programmed then listen to people's opinions. Does it sound like they've been plugged into the media line? Test yourself. Do you have firm views about people who you've never met in countries that you've never been to?

Even the freedom of the Internet is being assaulted. Sure it's reasonable to produce a programme to protect children from tacky pornographic sites. But if you dig deeper, some of this censor software also bans information about basic human rights. Feminism, contraception and gay and lesbian rights are out, as are sites featuring objectionable words. Some are so extreme that they border on the absurd.

An article in *.net* magazine says the following about a product called CYBERsitter: 'A site talking about single-sex schools or detailing a recipe for chicken breasts is likely to be blocked.' You have no choice about this. The software doesn't allow you to discern.

FREE YOUR SPIRIT

In isolation this may be acceptable, but when combined with high levels of negativity and other forms of information control it threatens our right to choose. The Bible tells us that God gave us freedom of choice and I believe that this is so because freedom is essential for our well-being. It gives us the opportunity to make decisions about who we are and what we're choosing to become. If we don't relinquish our individuality, we become independent and robust. Free people don't fear life. They are the most difficult for others to control. No one gave them their freedom. It's something they chose. They value it by being constructive and are able to make a difference to the world.

Richard Branson, the CEO of Virgin Airlines, is the person who for me epitomises personal freedom. He's had to deal with his fears, so can you. Like all of us Branson started his career with a host of insecurities. But instead of cowering behind them he turned self-doubt into a formidable motivating force. When he succeeded in taking British Airways on, he proved his insecurities wrong. No one controls him now, not even Inland Revenue. He pays his taxes, but never more than he has to. Nothing stops him either and his life is adventurous. He has fun.

If the things that scare you are important for your success, go out and do them anyway. Never let fear get in your way. Take baby-sized steps at first. If, for example, public speaking is high on your list, don't start with an audience of a hundred – try five or ten. Get comfortable with this and keep challenging your fear by moving on. Anyone can become a good orator. Just look at Anthony Robbins. Today he's one of the most highly paid speakers in the world. But in his book *Awaken the Giant Within*, he talks about his fear of public speaking. When his colleagues were doing two or three presentations a week he was doing the same number every day. Like everything else it takes lots of practice to cultivate a little talent and anyone can do this.

RAGE REVEALED

Never let fear or negativity compromise your individuality. If you do then understand from the messages of our emotions that compromising your priorities will make you angry. We have symptoms of this in our society. The Dunblaine massacre and school shoot-outs are evidence of abnormally high levels of rage. Anger mobilises us to fight and because of this it's critical that we learn to calm ourselves in more appropriate ways. Typically we respond to angry feelings by either stewing or exploding. Neither does us any good. Both just physically heat up the emotional brain and we continue to see red. However, the real risk of not dealing with our angry feelings is that eventually they will make us ill. In fact pent-up anger is thought to be twice as harmful to your health as chain-smoking!

When we feel angry there are a number of ways that we can respond. Firstly, in a heated situation call timeout. Get out before you say or do something that you may regret. Use this time to go through the following steps:

- ❖ read the message of your anger (from appendix 1)
- ❖ understand the compromise that you're facing
- ❖ make a decision about it
- ❖ act accordingly.

This will keep you rational and prevent an emotional hijacking.

Secondly, raging energy demands a hearing. Resist your temptation to explode. Instead write an angry letter to the person. Spew your rage onto the pages. Use the foulest language you wish and don't stop until you feel calm. Once you're through take your caustic pages to a safe place and burn them. The burning letter is a powerful symbol of your release. The first time you do this you may feel a bit foolish. Disregard it. Also bear in mind that you never ever send or keep an angry letter. If you want to communicate with the person involved, write an angry letter first, destroy it and only once the energy has been released talk or write to them.

Anger releases an overwhelming amount of energy. This is what makes us so destructive. Instead of harming someone else or damaging property, the third technique uses this energy constructively. It makes success your best revenge. Go out and show them. This is a great technique for dealing with angry resentments because it's one that will benefit you greatly.

Turning revenge into personal success has worked well for many South Africans who were damaged by the apartheid system. They know that it's futile to direct their angry energy at the old government. Nothing can change what happened and anger only keeps them stuck in the hopelessness of the past. Now many people are using their angry energy to drive their endeavours. Their need has catapulted their determination to prove the old system wrong and it's working.

DEPRESSION – UGH!

Anger happens when you feel that others have power over you and it has close links to depression. If you don't know how to deal with your anger appropriately you'll turn it inwards on yourself. If you do this, it'll make you more prone to giving in to the demands of others in future. Anger turned inwards feeds on your emotional resources and, unable to stand your ground, you'll eventually give in. Like the pike you get tired of bashing your head against the same wall and will probably find someone else to blame. Accusing others of making us miserable is a key characteristic of depression. It's maintained by the negative drain of energy, and being depressed confirms that we're no longer in control.

People-pleasers are the most prone to depression and women are particularly vulnerable. Janet was in her thirties when she consulted me about her depressive bouts. Her father had died a few years back and her mother was living with her aged aunt and uncle. Between them they could barely look after themselves.

'I get back from a hectic day at the office,' she said, 'rush over to cook their meal and come home exhausted. It frustrates me but what can I do? I've no choice but to care for them, after all they've taken my mother in.' More accurately she'd taken all three of them in, but she wasn't seeing this at the time.

Janet was single, lonely and down. Although she'd attempted a few relationships her partners wouldn't tolerate her family's demands. By the time she consulted me she was at the end of her rope. 'Now they've come up with a new idea. They want me to sell my apartment so that all four of us can buy a house together. I feel awful saying "no", but I can't handle it. It's already too much.' She was appalled at the thought of becoming a live-in nanny, but for her it was a *two-way lose*. She was damned if she complied and felt mean and uncaring if she didn't. Feeling fresh out of choices, she was stuck and very depressed.

Like Janet many people feel that they have no choice but to carry the burden of their depression. But Janet had a number of choices. The problem was that she had trapped herself. She didn't see that dealing with her own feelings was easier than having other people run her life. If she'd listened to the early warning signs, her frustration was telling her to change the situation. But for her change was not an option. It challenged her need to please. So instead she started an emotional battle with herself, waging war by silencing her feelings. She told herself that her needs weren't important and she was depleting her emotional energy by putting herself down. This made her feel even more hopeless.

By working through it Janet saw that this was the pattern of her life. Slowly she broke the habit by accepting her right to her own feelings and to having her needs met. She found good care for her family and visits now replace her mealtime chores. 'At first,' she says, 'it was hard. I felt terrible – much worse than they did. But when I was running around for them feeling resentful, depressed and angry, things were even more difficult.' By understanding how her need to please ensnared her in depression, she's now learnt to draw the line and this has changed her life.

If you suffer from bouts of depression, break this cycle by identifying what you need to do to retrieve your power. Spend time doing this because it may mean going back to assess what triggered the frustration initially. If you're able to identify the changes required, make some new decisions. These won't be easy to apply at first because the inability to confront these same issues sent you scuttling into depression in the past. Start with the little things – those that are easiest for you to deal with. Be creative; find new ways of handling these tricky situations. By tackling them step-by-step, each stage you conquer builds courage and will also arm you with some new tactics. Be brave; experiencing new strategies will build your inner strength and as you become stronger you'll eventually be able to face the bigger issues.

If you feel so immobilised that you're unable to address your depression, get help. Consult a psychologist or a minister or rabbi with counselling skills. Friends and family can't help you. They can only provide a sympathetic ear. Whatever you do, don't let the situation continue because depression robs you of life. It'll limit your choices and strip you of your freedom.

Knowing how to soothe anger, fear and depression makes us more resilient to the negative influences around us. These three emotions are powerful enough to sink us, but dealing with them maintains happiness as our normal state of mind. Being positive and optimistic keeps us in control because we know that we can rely on ourselves. This is relevant because it gives us full access to our inner resources.

RESOURCEFUL AND READY FOR LIFE

Resourceful individuals get on with the business of living. They make things happen. Unresourceful people sit on the sidelines – they watch. Like in any ball game, in life it's a sad reality that so many choose to spectate while few have opted to play.

What separates the two is the attitude driving our behaviour. Below you'll find a list of behaviours divided into two columns. Review your own over the past year. Which camp do you fall into? Whichever it is, your actions will dictate the outcome of your life.

Although being optimistic makes us resourceful, many people think it's about as beneficial as rearranging the deckchairs on the *Titanic*. But as a powerful buffer against negativity it's more like the life-raft that saves us. Let's face it – we either sink ourselves with the heavy weight of negativity or resist it by learning to swim. But the consequences of our decision have far broader reach. They go way beyond our own lives.

Resourceful states	Unresourceful states
Active	Aggressive
Confident	Apathetic
Constructive	Blaming
Effective	Critical
Energetic	Depressed
Fun-loving	Despair
Love	Frustration
Making a contribution	Destructive
Optimism	Helpless
Positive	Hopeless
Satisfied	Negative
Self-enrichment	Passive
Self-respect	Putting oneself down
Sociable	Struggling
Outcome	**Outcome**
Making it!	Losing out!

RICH ATTITUDES

Motivational author Wayne Dyer says, 'The state of the world reflects our state of mind,' and so does the state of our pocket. The economic repercussions of a nation drowning in negativity are severe. Economics has taken on a life of its own but in reality it's only about money – yours and mine. It's driven by confidence and this boils down to no more than our attitude. Optimism drives a boom, but the more pessimistic we are the deeper the recession we're plunged into. We believe it's beyond our control, yet our attitude is very much part of the force that drives it.

A smart businesswoman who wouldn't submit to a downturn taught me an important lesson in economic attitudes. For the five-year recession – while everyone else sat around discussing how bad things were – she doubled her substantial turnover every year. She disciplined herself to keep positive and found lots of new opportunities to make plenty of money. You can too.

If you think about it, some of the most successful businesses we know were initiated by the conditions of the Great Depression. Look at F W Woolworth. By packaging all goods into lots costing 5c each he could meet the slumping market's new demands. I'd bet that only by keeping positive did he come up with such a creative idea.

Knowledge keeps us buoyant and the more information that we have, the less frightening trying times appear. Don't believe the political-speak and economic jargon used to pull the wool over our eyes. If you listen to it, learn to read between the lines. Also master the art of the stupid question. Question everything you hear, read or see and don't stop until you get the information you need. Speak to lots of different people, study alternative opinions or get onto the Internet. Use whatever tools you have at your disposal. Knowledge bolsters you when you're up against negativity.

This is important because our mind has no preference for positive or negative thoughts. Either will do, but both are equally powerful in creating the circumstances of our lives. So not only do we need to be discerning about the information we allow into our mind, we also can't ignore our own thinking.

In the previous chapter we discussed turning negative thoughts into positive affirmations. Sales people I've worked with have had great results with this. A thought charged with lots of pessimistic emotion can sink us quickly. If you're in the middle of a negotiation it can mean no sale. Now, when sales people hear the negative noise they cling to the positives they've imprinted. This changes their attitude. It makes them more determined to win.

Another technique to eliminate negative thinking is laughter. Humour dissolves negativity. In business it can be a most helpful asset. Many years ago I read – in a women's magazine – a highly effective means of using humour to dissolve fear. If you're ever in a position where you have to conduct a presentation to high-status people and you feel in the slightest bit threatened or scared, picture each person in the audience sitting naked on the toilet. It's a great leveller and the amusement you'll create in your mind will also relax you and make the presentation lighter and more cheerful.

Fake feelings

Now what remains to be addressed are two emotions that drive us into negativity. These are worry and guilt. Both are fake feelings because they mask other emotions. If you look up the meaning of each in appendix 1 you'll see that guilt hides emotions that are unacceptable and worry is a veil for our real fears. Neither is productive and both waste time and energy. If you think about it, guilty feelings won't stop you from pursuing the same behaviour next time. Likewise worry doesn't change anything, it only keeps our mind focused on negative things.

The guilt trip

Guilt masks emotions we don't believe we have a right to feel. In a seminar this hit a delegate called Matthew right between the eyes. For eleven years guilt had kept him in an unsatisfactory relationship. 'In the beginning of our relationship I wasn't sure about Camilla. I'd told her how I felt and while we were seeing each other I dated other women. She put the pressure on, I gave in and we ended up together. Somehow she heard about one of my sexual escapades and, even after all these years, whenever we have a fight she throws this infidelity at me. She knew I felt guilty and now I can see how she's used it to manipulate me. If I'm cross with her I can't be angry because of the way I treated her before. Instead I've been doing guilt for so long.' When Matthew changed his behaviour Camilla was very unhappy. It took them six months of trying to work it out, but in the end they eventually parted.

Guilt usually hides feelings like resentment and anger. It's a decoy that's so consuming we forget about the real underlying feelings. But guilt doesn't change our behaviour: it just maintains the *status quo*. If you feel guilty about having an affair it won't stop you from seeing your lover. Nor will it address the problems in your marriage. It masks the real issues by trapping you in a guilt cycle. This can drive you to despair. Whenever you feel guilty, ask yourself, 'What feeling is guilt hiding from me?' Work with the underlying emotion because these masked feelings will give you accurate information. If you use it to resolve what's really troubling you, you'll overcome the guilty feeling.

WORRY, WORRY, WORRY

Worry also traps us because it seldom stops with a single thought. It triggers a stream of pessimistic ideas that escort your mind into the heart of negativity. This ensnares you in a cycle of distress. One thought leads to another and soon the events you've imagined have you paralysed with fear. If, for instance, your team leader calls you in before the meeting, you worry enough to convince yourself you're out of a job. But when reality doesn't confirm our worry we know it's hiding something. In this instance it's masking the fear of not being good enough.

Worry puts a mantle on our real concerns. While writing this, one of our cats became seriously ill and I kept saying to my husband, 'I'm so worried about her.' But worry wasn't what I was really feeling. More accurately, I was terrified for us. She's been such a joy in our lives that the thought of her dying was so difficult to confront. Worry maintains denial and it's unhealthy because it can also trigger guilt. We asked ourselves, 'Did we do enough?' and worried about this rather than deal with the real situation. (For other cat lovers out there, she miraculously survived!)

When faced with real concerns you'll need to deal with the underlying emotions, but mostly we worry over nothing. Learn to stop this pointless waste of energy by challenging the thought that triggered it. Ask yourself, 'Is this thought valid? Is it useful?' You'll usually find that it's a fabrication that serves little purpose. Then dig deeper to find out what you're really afraid of and work with that. If you hear it again, turn the thought into the opposite positive and repeat it as an affirmation. This way you'll stop yourself from imprinting negative beliefs. You'll also be positively tapping your power to create more constructive circumstances in future.

WAGE WAR

To eliminate pessimism from your life get into the habit of having days when you wage war on negativity. Start the morning with something pleasant. Listen to stirring music instead of the news. For breakfast delight yourself with an indulgence – you deserve it. Spend a little time thinking of the things that make you happy or satisfy your needs. Oprah Winfrey suggests starting a gratitude journal and this is a great way to push out negativity. As you're driving to work, instead of being consumed by the misery around you notice the beautiful flowers or remember a wonderful joke and smile.

During the day fight against negative thoughts. Also ignore pessimistic conversations or gently change the subject. Treat others to the best parts of yourself. Make them laugh, give genuine compliments and boost them. Put real quality into all of your relationships and during the day try befriending yourself.

If you encounter problems, deal with them as if they're opportunities to test your mettle. Be resourceful. Learn new things about yourself. Spend the day disproving your insecurities. Take on a new challenge no matter how big or small. Hear your emotions, deal with them and excite yourself with the successful results.

End the day by delighting in the sunset. Have a great meal. Go to a theatrical comedy, see an uplifting movie or read a book that stimulates you. Then check out how you feel. Are you more relaxed? Do you feel better about your life? Make a point of doing this regularly and soon you'll get into more positive life habits.

John-Roger and Peter McWilliams wrote an encouraging book with a terrific title: *You Can't Afford the Luxury of a Negative Thought*. No one can. Being negative is a choice you've made. It's a bad habit. Break it by dealing with the emotions that make you feel down and defy the thoughts that sink you. Resist it and you'll find that your physical health and mental and emotional well-being will improve. So will the state of your pocket. There's an old Chinese proverb that says, 'We can't help the birds of sadness flying over our heads, but we need not let them build nests in our hair.' Apply this to negativity and soon you'll be back in the driving seat of your life.

Growing up

People who had been bankrupted at least once were prime candidates for management positions when Bill Gates started Microsoft. One wonders how such a successful business could've been built on the back of other people's failures. 'Surely,' we protest, 'if they couldn't manage their own concern what can they contribute now?' But there was method in Gates's seeming madness. People who've made a come-back from personal devastation are strengthened by the experience. If they've picked themselves up from failure once, they'll never fear it again. They can take risks because they've proved to themselves that they can rely on their own resources.

Contrary to popular belief, the road to success is paved with many failures. Failure is one of life's most powerful teachers; and dodging it amounts to avoiding the chance to be successful. Tolerating personal failure makes us emotionally hardy because every time we bounce back we stretch our resources. In this way failure sows the seeds of our success because it shows us more about who we are. It tests our commitment, draws out resources like our creative spirit, determination and inner strength. These are essential tools for future achievement and failure teaches us about them.

So essential is experiencing failure that it could be said that if you've never had any spectacular botch-ups, you'll have missed the lessons that could turn you into a sensational success. Virtually every success story we know is about someone who's been in the doldrums at least once in their lives.

Many famous actors have waited tables, even emptied trash cans; and Walt Disney was thought to have gone bankrupt seven times before his legend became a reality.

Even the clever invention of the photostat machine was rejected by more than 20 companies before the business we now know as Xerox finally took it on. If the inventor Chester Carlson hadn't persisted, we might still be using those messy old Roneo machines.

Being in the doldrums is not a sign of personal failure but staying stuck there is. What makes the difference is not the failures themselves but how we deal with them. How we explain our mistakes and flops is relevant. If we tell ourselves that we failed because of some deep flaw, we'll never get on top of the challenges we face.

This is so because our belief in our own inadequacy just keeps sinking us. But if we accept each mistake and learn from it, we gain the knowledge to act more intelligently in any new undertaking.

Learning and growing from our experiences moves us into maturity in our adult lives. It is the essence of becoming emotionally intelligent. People with healthy levels of EQ make a habit of addressing life's lessons as they graduate through the various stages of emotional development. They've learnt to become emotionally fit. Now they are robust people.

Emotional development happens in the following five stages and growth depends on our ability to learn the lessons from all of our experiences. These stages are appropriate at certain ages, but some people grow faster and mature quite young while others stay stuck and may never reach the final stages.

ACCEPTANCE

In the early stage of our life we know that our emotional brain dominates our existence. It means that we accept whatever we're told and any thoughts repeated are believed to be true. This forms the beginning of our self-image and world-view. It's the baseline for who we believe we are. It also cements beliefs about the impact that we think we can have on the society around us.

When we're in the acceptance stage our opinions are not our own. They're a conglomerate of other people's views. If we're repeatedly told that we're gifted, special and lovable, we'll act that way. Equally true, if others tell us that we're stupid, lazy and problematic, we'll prove these opinions correct too. Because we cannot yet discern about the information we receive, we act like sponges absorbing everything around us. If the water is clean, we grow up in a healthy environment. If it's muddied with helplessness or cynicism, our young minds will be polluted with the same beliefs.

At this early stage we model ourselves on the adults around us. We don't do as they say but watch and mimic what they do. So how they behave will form our early patterns. If our parents or care-givers couldn't control their emotions, neither will we. If they are deviously manipulative, we'll also use similar behaviour to get our own way. On the other hand if we see our parents taking responsibility for themselves, we learn healthy tools for our own survival.

From our significant others we also learn either to hope or despair about our future. Whenever parents consistently adopt a negative view they teach their children that life is hopeless. But if other people are motivated and excited about their lives, their children learn to be resourceful. Children like to be around adults because every time they listen to grown-up experiences they gather new tools for themselves. In their childlike way they apply these skills to their own lives.

The degree to which our parents believed in themselves also dictated their belief in us. It'll determine whether we're comfortable with ourselves later on. If your parents liked and respected who they are, it's likely that you'll feel the same way about who you've become. But critical parents do the opposite. They showed you your flaws and made these the focus of your adult attention.

When our development is arrested we stay stuck at this stage. Behaviours which may be appropriate for children become our way of dealing with obstacles and difficulties in our adult lives. Look at this list of age-appropriate behaviours for children and the corresponding list of adult symptoms. These are symptomatic of being stuck at the acceptance stage.

Age-appropriate behaviours	Adult symptoms
(Beneficial behaviours marked *)	
Bullying	Blaming
Creative *	Critical
Curious *	Depressed
Demanding	Prone to frequent emotional hijackings
Energetic *	Helpless
Prone to frequent tears	Manipulative
Innocent *	Negative/pessimistic
Playful *	Passive aggressive/resistance
Resourceful *	Speak without thinking
Speak without thinking	Making unrealistic demands
Temper tantrums	Unresourceful
Whining	Victim behaviour

When as adults we retain the beneficial aspects of childhood and learn from the others, we integrate the child within. This allows us to take these assets into the next stage of our growth. However, if your development has been unhealthy, as an adult you'll still use the negative aspects of childhood to manipulate your world. These are listed as the adult symptoms.

Some people use childish manipulations because they believe that these behaviours work. A manager in a company I consulted to asked my advice about a difficult staff member he worked with. Patricia had a problem with authority. Her performance was average and he knew that she could achieve much more. 'Whenever we talk about it or I put pressure on her,' he said, 'she gets into a rage and screams and shouts about how I'm taking advantage of her.'

When I asked about what happened after Patricia's emotional hijacking he told me that he usually gave in to her. Obviously Patricia was using her dependent behaviour to manipulate him. She knew that she would get her own way by having an outburst. For the first few times it had worked, but now he was fed up and had lost interest. Patricia's behaviour had become transparent and, rather than co-operating with her, colleagues mostly avoided her. So her behaviour may have produced short-term results, but it won't help her to fulfil any long-term goals.

If some of the adult symptoms ring true for you it means that, like Patricia, you haven't yet learnt from your childhood experiences. Because you lack this vital knowledge you can't move on. If you're stuck in dependency, know that as an adult your parents no longer control you – only you do. And if their words still rule, understand that they only exist in your head. You can change them by shifting your thinking. Take responsibility by gaining control of your mind. Use the emotional and mind power tools that have been detailed so far. They'll help you to take charge of your life in future.

REBELLION

Questioning moves us out of the acceptance phase and into the teenage rebellion. It's healthy because it means that we're learning to test our thinking and stand on our own two feet. We move into this stage when we realise that we haven't been told the truth about ourselves. We start to question our self-image and world-view. One query leads to another and the world as we've known it through other people's eyes begins to crumble.

It's a time of self-discovery; and the more we disprove our negative thinking and childlike insecurities, the more we learn about who we are. Instead of taking other people's opinions at face value we start reshaping our own character and begin exploring life for ourselves.

The movement from acceptance to rebellion usually occurs when we're away from the people who dominated us. We drop the super-hero status we assigned to our parents and test their world-view against our own experiences. Instead of complying with other people's beliefs we take risks (sometimes foolishly) and challenge ourselves. No matter how much this may terrify you as a parent, understand that a healthy rebellion is always a sign of your child's positive development.

The rebellion is the first stage in learning to be street-wise. It's an experimental time and no book can teach us the life-skills we learn from experience. By facing the consequences of our actions we become aware of behaviours that work for or against us. The more mistakes we make and the more pain we feel, the greater the likelihood of eradicating ineffective aspects of our behaviour. Each success we have is a notch on our belt and we build on these to create bigger and better achievements in future. In a nut-shell, rebellion shows us how we can operate in our world.

People who for whatever reason don't experience this stage seldom have a deep understanding of who they are. A woman I knew many years ago fell into this category. When Laura was 17 her parents got divorced and this was the factor that more than likely arrested her development. Her mother was deeply distressed and, from what Laura said, sounded on the verge of a breakdown.

'Mum was so upset for so long and I can remember her crying for days on end. My brothers and I tried everything, but nothing that we did cheered her up. I even felt bad going away to college and leaving her, but my father insisted.' This continued for a number of years and Laura made it her business to look after her mother when she could. Even many years later when Laura emigrated her mother joined her after just a few months.

Deep down Laura believed that any rebellion would have added to the family's distress. By the time I met her she was 29 and dissatisfied with her life. She had had many months of voluntary unemployment because she was bored with the career she'd chosen. At the time I suggested therapy and Laura went along. After a few sessions we reconnected and she told me, 'The shrink wanted to know if I'd ever rebelled against anything and I was amazed that there wasn't a single thing that I could think of. She suggested that I start now.'

Laura had always been the sort of person to comply with other people's needs. It didn't matter whether the unreasonable demands were being made by her mother, lover or boss – she would submit to them. At 29 she was stuck in the acceptance stage and would go along unwillingly, feeling miserable in the process. Instead of rebelling she'd get depressed and when she couldn't take it anymore, she'd simply walk away.

To my knowledge Laura has still never indulged in a healthy rebellion and the last time I saw her she'd just left another job without having any idea of her next step. Now she's 36 and has a four-year-old child, so the stakes are higher. The tragedy is that other people see Laura as a highly intelligent person whose many talents could be applied to achieving great things in her life. If only for a little rebellion so that she could see this for herself.

The other side of this coin is people who never leave the rebellious stage. They're stuck because they've developed habits that may have worked for them when they were teenagers, but which are no longer tolerable in adult life. Paul, a training delegate, first rebelled against his father. He was adamant about not continuing his education, which is what his father wanted him to do. Instead he got a job. After being dismissed numerous times he started his own business.

Paul is highly creative, but he can't seem to sustain success. 'Whenever things start going well, something goes wrong. I think I've just got shit for luck,' he told me. When we delved into his behaviour it wasn't luck that was at issue here. Paul's problem was that he couldn't stand being told what to do. In his business he was often let down by contractors; and because he was still rebelling his demanding clients got short shrift from him. This obviously affected repeat business and referrals; and to get each new contract Paul virtually had to start again.

His need to rebel against any form of authority also meant that the financial side of his business was in disarray. Keeping up-to-date records was a little too formal for this rebellious 32-year-old and he regularly had problems with Inland Revenue.

To assist Paul I drew on the example of Richard Branson. He's revolutionised many industries and made his rebellion work constructively for him. He didn't give in nor did he fight against anyone. Instead Branson's rebellious energy became his point of leverage. Staid competitors can't compete with his innovative ideas and he's used these successfully to work his way to the top.

Once Paul could see that his teenage rebellion had carried into his adult life he started to change his attitude. Instead of fighting he's learnt more mature social skills and now handles his clients and contractors more appropriately. He also addresses problems before they reach a crisis; and rather than bumping his head against the same brick wall he's learning from his mistakes. His view of success has also changed. Whereas previously he had believed that achievements would play into his father's hands, he released himself from failure by reframing his thoughts. Now he's doing it for himself. He's also integrated his revolutionary energy and today is challenging big competitors with his imaginative concepts. So far it's working out great for him.

Age-appropriate behaviours	Adult symptoms
(Beneficial behaviours taken through from acceptance stage marked *; beneficial rebellion stage behaviour marked †)	

Age-appropriate behaviours	Adult symptoms
Anti-social	Arguments
Arguments/aggression	Attention-seeking
Attention-seeking	Bravado
Creative *	Disorganised
Challenging authority	Egocentric
Curious *	Critical
Deception	Embellishing
Eccentricity	Lacking commitment
Energetic *	Low frustration tolerance
Inability to understand consequences	Need to be right
Innocent *	Negative
Irresponsible	Needing to shock
Playful *	Pessimistic
Questioning †	Poor social skills
Resourceful *	Self-involvement
Uncontrollable anger	Self-righteousness
Not punctual	Not punctual

The ability to question is the greatest gift of our rebellious years. If we question our own thoughts and behaviours our growth is turbo-boosted. When we query our world-view we start making the world a more manageable place. This takes us to the next stage of our adult development: transparency.

TRANSPARENCY

The workings of the world become transparent when we increase our knowledge base. As we start to decipher the bigger picture of life, things that may have confused or overwhelmed us become more manageable.

We get to this stage by learning from our life-experiences and coming up with new ideas. It's about exploring our adult curiosity and can mean lots of reading and research into the things that inspire us. We usually enter this stage in our late twenties or early thirties.

Here little holds us back because we've learnt to manage our power and manoeuvre most situations to our advantage. We have an abundance of social skills, are in control of our emotions and are free to test any new ideas. This increases our confidence and life becomes a playground for our success. Most people at this stage are settling into careers they love and their labour is no longer a toil. It becomes the means to express themselves and they take great pride in what they deliver.

People at the transparency stage are emotionally robust, they can take knocks because they know how to bounce back and revive themselves. They also know how to get their own needs met. They ask openly rather than manipulating other people. They're outspoken about their ideas and don't take rejection personally.

People who reach this stage have happiness as their baseline. They deal with their fears, seldom get down and no one controls them but themselves. They seek out information to feed their inquisitive minds; and nothing stimulates them more than new thinking that they can apply to their own lives. People who make the world transparent are also interesting. They discuss ideas rather than gossip and usually leave you with something you can learn from. They do so because they care deeply about people. This caring takes them through to the next stage of contribution.

Age-appropriate behaviours

(These are adult behaviours so there are no age-inappropriate behaviours)
(Acceptance stage behaviours marked *; Rebellion stage
behaviour marked †)

Care (people, environment, themselves)
Creative *
Curious *
Emotional fitness/control
Energetic *
Enthusiasm
Flexibility
Fun
Innocent *
Innovation
Inspiring
Intimacy
Inquisitiveness
High level of social skills
Love of life
Playful *
Positive/optimistic
Questioning †
Resourceful *
Spontaneity
Warmth

CONTRIBUTION

In chapter 3 we discussed how happiness directs our energy outwards and how we can use this to make a contribution to life. It
can only happen through our experiences and we get to this
stage by growing through the ones preceding it. There is no
shortcut because the tools that we need here are learnt during
previous stages. Making a contribution will be explored in depth

in the following two chapters. What's important for now is to know that you won't get to this rewarding stage unless you're mentally and emotionally prepared for it. Any adult at any age can work through acceptance and rebellion. If you don't yet feel prepared, use the tools in this book to do so.

The forties usually heralds the time when we start actively making a difference. We're no longer plagued by childhood difficulties and have a profound understanding of our world. Usually we'll fluctuate between stages three and four gaining more knowledge to apply to the success of our endeavours. We keep growing and learning and this takes us through to retirement.

WISDOM

This is the final stage in our growth quest. It's the stage where we're comfortable with the contribution we've made and can relax into the last stages of life. It's a time of deep contentment and satisfaction and often of great sharing.

In ancient cultures like the Aboriginals, Native Americans and Africans wise older people are the ones who are most revered. Youngsters consult them and the advice they give is backed by their years of experience. People at this stage of life know better than to dictate or prescribe. They merely share what they've learnt so that others may gain from their lives.

It's a sad reality in our Western world that we have little use for old people. We dismiss any wisdom they have as old fuddy-duddy stuff. We have a preference for youth; but their rebellious ideas are only useful if we want to shake things up. Often without the bigger picture or a longer-term view, our answers tend to be quick fixes rather than permanent solutions.

My father's life-experience taught me a valuable lesson. In my rebellion stage I firmly believed that I could fast-track success. Wealth was a high priority and I worked day and night to make it. After I had suffered innumerable stress-related illnesses he told me about the importance of enjoying the journey.

His own stress had interfered with his ability to savour his success. He was sowing the seeds of experience; by combining this with my own lessons from many more stress-related problems, enjoying the journey is now the priority of my life. His path was completely different to mine, but still his life lessons were very valuable to my existence.

Life offers a university of experiences; and the more we learn from our own experiences or those of other people, the higher the qualification we get. Like school, good grades shift us to the next level of development where we are rewarded with more and more success. To qualify we need to capitalise on the energy of our successes and keep focused on reviewing our mistakes and failures. How we deal with mistakes and failures determines our stage of growth; and when it comes to coping with them we can go one of three ways.

THE BLAME GAME

The first option is blame. From the previous chapter we know that blaming other people makes us hand over the controls. We lose power because if the fault lies with someone else we're unable to change the situation. Also blaming a flaw in ourselves means that we've succumbed to our inadequacies. Either way robs us of our ability to respond. By dodging 'response-ability' we feel helpless and this path has only one destination – depression. It keeps us in the acceptance stage and instead of mastering our own destiny we become a victim of other people's choices.

A BBC documentary detailing the nomadic lives of Russians who breed reindeer provides a refreshing example of people who refused to be victimised. For them the end of communism meant a withdrawal of government support. Their lives are tough, but even so one of the women philosophically said, 'We accept it because it's the way things are.' These people know that blaming the government is as futile as trying to change the icy weather. Sitting around feeling sorry for themselves would also be useless. Only by acknowledging their situation were they able to respond. They've now mustered their resources and are surviving in a more challenging commercial environment.

If you're in a situation where you feel unable to take charge of your own life, you can do the same. Accept the circumstances that you're in and make a plan to work around them. Nobody ever needs to be stuck in helplessness. You only feel it because blame blocks access to your inner resources. It gets you so wrapped up in resentment, anger or self-pity that you stop thinking about solutions that could help. But there are always things that you can do to respond.

Start by scrutinising who you're blaming and why. If it's yourself, examine the inadequacies you've come to believe. You'll probably find that they're lies from rerunning old negative thinking.

Next make a list of all the things you can do to change your situation. Even if some items on your list seem silly, don't worry because they'll help to get your creative juices flowing. Out of the list identify possible solutions and act on them. At first it may not work out one hundred per cent right. Like the Russian nomads, keep learning from your experiences. This knowledge will assist you to fine-tune your solution. Don't stop working at it until you achieve the outcome you want.

UNCOMFORTABLE COMFORT ZONES

The second option for dealing with failure is best explained by an example cited by Stephen Covey in his book *The Seven Habits of Highly Effective People*. He quotes a case study of an employee who retired after 17 years of service. To replace him the business management set out to analyse what he did. On close inspection they found that he'd done one year's work 17 times over.

This is a nine-to-five existence and if it's where you fit in, understand that a comfort zone offers no risks, few challenges and little stimulation. Bored people are boring. They keep doing the same thing and duplicating the same mediocre results. Break the pattern by making different decisions to shake up your routine. Here any decision is better than no decision. After all, the worst that can happen is that a wrong decision will teach you something new about yourself. This is important because, in this the age of imagination, jaded nine-to-fivers are unlikely to get very far.

LEARN TO EARN

Success doesn't just happen to people. It's a reward for gaining lots of life experience along the way. Knowledge + experience = wisdom and from the research into EQ we know that the street-wise succeed. They use mistakes and failures to arm themselves with a munition of life experiences. This protects them from having to repeat the same mistakes again. It moves them forward.

For me Tina Turner's life story epitomises this and shows us the third option for dealing with failure. Given the abusive circumstances of her marriage to Ike she could easily have collapsed into the victim role. She also could've believed him when he repeatedly said that she was mediocre. Instead, over the years Turner systematically demanded more and more from herself. She did so by going through the painful process of watching videotapes of each of her performances. This provided her with the insight to introduce new aspects into and eradicate bad habits from her show. She kept challenging her level of professionalism and today the results more than speak for themselves.

If you can objectively study the results you've produced, you're free to modify the decisions you've made. There is a good reason for every outcome; and reviewing it non-emotionally arms you with fresh ideas and necessary information for a successful result in future. This is the mark of the emotionally mature person. Instead of allowing disappointments and bad feelings to drain their power they read and respond to the message of their emotions. They constantly modify their behaviour and by doing so they move into the transparency stage, which prepares them for a successful contribution.

You'll see that this is true if you recall the experience of going through your driving test. You knew that if you didn't study or practise your skills, you couldn't expect to pass. If you failed and said to yourself, 'I'm too stupid to learn to drive,' you'd never have been rewarded with a licence. Also, blaming the instructor would've made you helpless to change the situation. Only by re-taking the test and learning from your mistakes did you get through it successfully later. The same applies to life. Success happens when we apply the knowledge we've gained to our current experiences.

MISTAKES MOTIVATE

In the school of life, develop a tolerance for mistakes and flopped ventures. They are our most powerful teachers. Unlike successes, flops force us to stop and review our attitude and behaviour. If you've ever paid life's school fees with your own pain, you'll know that anguish drives us to learn from our experiences. This is why we gain more feedback from failed ventures than we do from our accomplishments. Bouncing back gives us the opportunity to make new decisions about who we are, but achievements mostly maintain our existing habits. If you're comfortable with the level of success you've reached then this is perfectly acceptable. But if you're not, you'll need to take on more risks and challenges. After all, bomb-proofing your ass from the peril of mistakes only keeps you stuck in mediocrity or failure.

To avoid this go back in your life now and remember some of your failures. They'll still hurt if you haven't yet learnt all the lessons from them. Stop now and think what these experiences taught you. Why are you better off today from having had these painful episodes? How did they equip you to manage life as you experience it currently?

If you think that they didn't benefit you in any way then it's likely that staying stuck in your pain could suit you. Perhaps your misery is a powerful tool you're using to manipulate other people. But understand that the more hardships you've learnt from, the better equipped you are to face success in future. The lesson may not always be apparent immediately. Just keep asking the question and eventually the answer will come.

When it comes to growth it's distressing that we live in a culture that denies mistakes and failures.

At the time of writing, Bill Clinton's denial of his extramarital affairs was all over the news. If he'd just admitted it earlier, great costs could have been saved by the American nation. But in our lives when we sweep our mistakes under the carpet the costs are not only financial.

Hiding important life lessons from ourselves inhibits our growth because we limit the amount of information we have to work with. It's often the cause of our falling short of our full potential. Yet every time we review the full extent of each mistake we've made, we turn a messy situation into valuable qualifications from the university of experience.

To have a tool for reviewing your progress you may want now to turn to appendix 3 where you'll find a questionnaire to help you. Use it regularly to update your progress and keep you focused on growth. This will ensure that your life is on track to reap the rewards of wisdom when you finally close the chapter.

The meaning
of life

On my grandmother's 97th birthday I was telling her what an important role she'd played in the early part of my life. Although by then she was very frail she replied, 'I'm so pleased dear, because before I can die I need to know that my life has been valuable to other people.' The phrase 'before I can die' really struck me because it corresponded so closely with one of the core issues of emotional intelligence. To know that our existence has made a difference is a fundamental need in all of us. It gives our lives purpose and when we satisfy this yearning to make a meaningful contribution we feel fulfilled and gratified.

Gail Sheehy in her book *Pathfinders* confirms this. She claims, 'My research offers impressive evidence that we feel better when we attempt to make our world a better place.' We discussed previously that our spiritual side generates power from our soul and this energy is managed by our emotions. So if we're channelling this force into a meaningful contribution, the sense of fulfilment that we feel keeps pumping up our energy. This is why living one's purpose is motivating. It generates more and more energy to create greater and greater success.

On the other hand, if we believe that we're not useful, our life becomes empty and this often strikes us in the transparency stage of our growth. It's commonly called a mid-life crisis and many people who hit it profoundly question what life is all about. For some the emptiness is so overwhelming that they resign themselves to it for the rest of their lives. For others it's a big wake-up call inspiring them to use their existence to make a difference now. Up until the transparency stage the more unaware of this human need we've been, the harder it knocks us when it creeps up. So no matter what stage you're currently at, understanding this need and preparing yourself for it will ease the challenge when it arrives. And you can be sure that it will!

REBEL WITH A CAUSE

The tools that we use to make a contribution are found in the rebellion stage of our growth. Rebellion tests our individuality, and only by drawing upon our uniqueness can we satisfy our distinctive purpose in life. And we all have one. Of course not everyone is destined to be a movie star, a world-renowned artist or the president of the United States. People who take on these jobs are expressing their unique talents and putting their personal stamp on life as only they know how.

Instead think of success in a broader sense. The great philosopher Ralph Waldo Emerson would define you as being successful 'If just one life has breathed easier because you have lived'. So your purpose, like my grandmother's, may not have anything to do with fame or fortune. It may be about being happy, raising well-adjusted children or helping others in your own quiet way. Any of these is a great achievement and each would leave a terrific legacy in your wake.

In the latter part of Michael Caine's career he was asked why he had chosen to play so many diverse movie roles. He replied, 'Well, I just wanted a few people on the planet to know that I was here.' People will remember you either because you contributed to their existence or you irritated them intensely. How do you want to be remembered? Test yourself now by writing down a list of at least ten people whose lives you've added value to over the past year. These are some of the reasons they'll know that you existed. It doesn't matter whether you judge the contribution to be big or small, add each item to the list. Once you're through check how you feel. If you've struggled to find a minimum of ten, does this correspond to any feelings of emptiness that you may have?

Idle Worship

We know that the need to make a contribution emerges from our spiritual life; and here I'm not necessarily referring to religion but more broadly to our hunger for meaning. If we don't find it in our own lives, our natural desire often coaxes us to create idols for our own 'worship'.

It's worth a thought that our need to believe in something bigger than ourselves may power our insatiable appetite for scandals about stars in Hollywood, big business, football, cricket, golf, rugby and you-name-it.

I was in the UK shortly after Princess Diana's funeral and it's not insignificant that the words on everyone's lips were 'My, but her coffin was small!' We made her larger than life and were surprised to discover that she was the same size as everyone else. This human need is so strong that behaviour not too dissimilar to some spiritual rituals of our ancestors can also be seen in sports supporters. Fans dress in team colours, paint their faces and commonly perform all sorts of strange physical rites. The Mexican Wave is a good example where repetitive chants – powerful enough to get groups into a frenzied, trance-like state – fuel actions.

It's also relevant that the game is no longer a game. Now with nastier elements like football hooliganism it's literally become a matter of life and death – a crusade that some admit ranks higher in their lives than anything else. Supporters will say that team wins give their lives meaning and that games can take priority over family, career and any other personal commitments.

Whether it's mourning for a princess few ever knew or the wild actions of a football supporter, these behaviours are symptoms of our search for meaning. If our own lives are devoid of purpose, we often transfer this need onto other people. But does it really let us off the hook?

JUST DO IT!

Dr David Lewis in his book *10 Minutes Time and Stress Management* reports that there are four categories into which most people's lives fit:

- ❖ 30% are inactive. They have no goals and act only when told what to do. They've not grown beyond the acceptance stage because dependency and depression keep them here.
- ❖ 50% are reactive. These people respond to change, but don't initiate it nor take control of their own destiny. Fear keeps them stuck in acceptance.
- ❖ 10% are dreamers. People here may be full of good ideas, but fail to take the practical steps needed to make their dreams reality. They are scattered and stuck in rebellion.
- ❖ 10% are proactive. They make things happen. People in this category move through transparency into contribution and wisdom.

Where do you fit in? Anyone can join the proactive group and make things happen. It's not a matter of being especially gifted; it's about how you manage your energy. Like them you can do whatever it takes to make things happen your way. Successful people are living their contribution now and there's no reason why you can't be one of them. Just imagine how exciting our world would be if the percentages above were reversed. All of our lives would be different if 90 per cent of the population was fulfilled by their proactive contribution and only ten per cent made up the other three low-energy groupings.

WHAT WILL YOUR OBITUARY READ?

If you're not yet a paid-up member of the proactive group, think about this: how would you feel if you died tomorrow? What could you claim that your life had contributed? I've heard numerous people who have terminal diseases say, 'I feel sorry for people who don't know that they're dying because they don't know how to live.' Whether we accept it or not, the truth is that we're all dying, most of us just don't know when.

David Patient, a South African who was diagnosed as being HIV-positive in 1982, can't afford to take life for granted. His case has been researched internationally and there's no conclusive proof that anything but a great attitude has kept the full-blown disease at bay. In an interview he was asked what the future holds and he said, 'I don't know. I just wake up in the morning and if I'm still breathing I know it's going to be a fabulous day!' How many of us can say we even notice that we're breathing?

All these years later David looks extremely healthy and now runs workshops for other sufferers. But his history shows that the turnaround didn't happen immediately. His first reaction was to escape his fear by dabbling with drugs. After surfacing from the fog of his addiction he decided to deal with death by getting on with the business of living.

Now he's turned his life-threatening condition into a most valuable contribution. What's so fascinating about his story is that, as so often happens, his purpose emerged from a deeply distressing situation. Perhaps without the sword of Damocles over his head he may not have discovered how powerful he could become.

DEATH DEFYING

There's nothing like the threat of death to motivate us to make the most of living. It focuses us on our sense of purpose and the more we're aware of it the more proactive we become. On a fun television show hosted by one of the Two Ronnies, children were asked if they wanted to live forever. One of them said, 'I don't think so because what would there be to live for?' Ask yourself the question to find out what you're living for right now.

Not so long ago my husband and I went walking with friends in the mountains. It was a walk that considerably challenged our fear of heights, something we all suffer from. Once back with our feet firmly planted on even ground we laughed as we toasted the goodness of life. One of our friends who'd been overwhelmed with fear piped up. 'Yeah,' he sighed, 'it feels real good to be alive! And isn't it funny how we complain about it all the time!' If you knew that you were going to exit the planet tomorrow, what would you stop complaining about today?

Also, what do you think that you may regret most? The fact that you didn't make more money or that you failed to create a life that was valuable to other people? Think deeply about this question because the regrets you believe you may have will point out what's meaningful to you right now. Instead of risking remorse, act with urgency because you may not be capable of fulfilling these needs later.

Older people will often tell you that they regret the things they didn't do, not the things they did. They've learnt the value of experiences and now wish that they hadn't allowed fear to stop them from making the most of every moment. Like them, fear and dependency will keep you from making your unique contribution. Don't let these feelings inhibit your progress. Think about being at the end of your life. Wouldn't it be soul-destroying to regret not having made the most of your existence?

ADDING VALUE

Being satisfied in life is a function of, firstly, adding value to our relationships and, secondly, being challenged by all manner of experiences. It's not so much what we get out of them, but more what we put in. The rewards we reap are in direct proportion to the contribution we make; and when we continuously add to our own lives we contribute much to the people around us. If you build on both your experiences and relationships, at the end you'll be able to justifiably say, 'What a fantastic life I've had!' After all, the wealth of our relationships and the wisdom from our experiences are the only things that we can take with us when we die.

Be aware that life isn't going to land excitement and satisfaction in our laps. It's there, but we have to go out and find it. This is the difference between those who are proactive and those who aren't. The experiences of proactive people have revealed who they uniquely are and they build upon their individuality to contribute in their own special way. Proactive people see their lives as a work in progress, one that they're constantly changing. So can you.

THE ART OF LIVING

Every person's life is an unfinished masterpiece; and to enrich the picture you need to have a clear idea of what you want to create on the canvas. Having a mission will keep you focused on what's important; and with the distractions of our hi-tech world this is probably more important now than ever before. Changing times expose untold new opportunities; and having a mission makes it easier to make the right life-changing decisions. A personal mission gives us something to test new ventures against. If it fits, we can be confident that this particular new challenge will keep us living on purpose. If it doesn't, pursuing it could mean losing sight of our original mission.

For example, my own mission is to be a messenger for re-creation. It involves empowering other people. But as my first career was marketing I also have many skills in this area. These skills are valuable to me now. But if I was approached to produce a series of catalogues for a clothing manufacturer – I could do it – it would distract me from my current purpose. This would scatter my energy making it that much harder to get back on track once the job was over.

WHAT DO YOU WANT?

Having a clear idea of what you want is the first step to being proactive. Our purpose is our passion; and knowing what we want means that we can paddle our own canoe. Having a mission provides stability which is necessary when life ambushes us with the inevitable surge of surprises. When we don't know where we're heading the river of life can dump us on an embankment anywhere. This wastes time as we struggle to get back to wherever we came from. But when we know the destiny that we desire, we can paddle directly into our own future.

If you're unsure of your mission, follow the steps in this chapter to get a firmer idea. The benefits to you are so great that I urge you to keep working at it until you've developed a very clear idea of your life-path in future. As you work through the steps remember that your mind knows what your life-purpose is. So it's not something that you need to create, but something that you need to discover. To uncover it you'll need to work through the exercises on page 116 and make time for lots of self-reflection. Don't worry if you find that it's a struggle; wrestling with yourself is normal with any form of self-analysis. Be patient and keep drawing on your unlimited resources.

The mission that you choose needs to be broad enough to cater for all eventualities along your life-path. For instance, my own allows for being a messenger by conducting seminars, writing books, producing videos or using all sorts of electronic media. Certainly this will keep me off the streets for a while, but it could potentially include a career in politics. In the same way your mission needs to guide your choices. That's why saying something like 'I want to be happy and successful' is not enough. This isn't a mission: it's a want or a desire. A mission must provide you with some indication of who you need to be to be happy for the rest of your life. It must be an expression of who you're choosing to become.

It doesn't matter what your contribution is but it will reward you greatly if it emerges from your individuality. If your mission is fulfilled by your current occupation, don't be disheartened by the fact that thousands of other people may be working in similar careers. It's about you being the very best that you can be and how you use this to add value to your field of work.

SELF-ANALYSIS

The process starts with an analysis of who you are now. Different circumstances draw out different aspects of our character; and analysing these gives us a good idea of the different faces that we show to the world. It will reveal the many qualities that you have. When completing this section avoid glib labels like secretary, accountant, mother or father, because they won't tell you anything about who you are. Instead use adjectives – words that describe your behaviour.

1. Who are you when you're at home? Are you relaxed, uptight, kind, bad-tempered etc?

_____

_____

_____

_____

2. What type of person are you at work?

_____

_____

_____

3. What type of person are you when you're with your original family (parents, siblings)?

_____

_____

_____

4. Who are you when you're with your friends?

_____

_____

_____

5. Who are you in your community (clubs, charity work, church groups, PTA, etc.)?

_____

_____

_____

6. Who are you when you're alone?

_____

_____

_____

This exercise will provide you with a broad picture of the foundation for who you want to become. Review what you've written to explore the varied sides of yourself. Which aspects are you most comfortable with?

Next let's go a little deeper. The more information that you put down for each category the easier it will be to get to your personal mission statement.

1. What are your interests?

_____

What types of books stimulate you?

_____

What types of movies appeal to you?

_____

What types of TV programmes do you most enjoy?

_____

What types of magazines do you read?

_____

2. Do you have any hobbies?

_____

_____

_____

3. Identify your talents and gifts (things that you do naturally well).

_____

_____

_____

4. Identify your most important skills (things that you've learnt to do).

_____

_____

_____

5. What are you good at and what do you like doing? (These are your strengths.)

_____

_____

_____

6. Identify your weaknesses or the things that you don't like doing.

_____

_____

_____

7. What would you like to be doing in the future? What are your ambitions?

_____

_____

_____

Examine the lists that you've made here. If you're relatively happy about life, you should see similarities throughout, except for question 6 which addresses your weaknesses. If your area of skill is totally out of kilter with the rest and it's your job, it could be an indication that your career is outside of your area of passion. Instead of packing in your job look at how you could employ the skills that you've learnt in areas that have more natural appeal to you. Can you integrate them into a life-purpose that's more meaningful? It's possible if you draw on your creative thinking ability.

This is exactly what Peter Franklin did. Better known as New York's 'Gabby Cabby', he is evidently more passionate about his city than driving a cab. But his mobility allows him to meet the people who give New York its unique quirks and flavour. With his interesting insights, he weekly entertains millions of people over dozens of radio stations worldwide. If you think about it, all cab drivers are exposed to this, but how many other New York cabbies are known globally? Starting out in the same way as all other cab drivers, Franklin needed a good creative spark, backed by a proactive drive, to make his valuable contribution to the world.

To find your passion review the analysis you've completed so far and look for the elements that make you most enthusiastic. It's interesting that the stem of the word 'enthusiasm' is *entheos* meaning inspired by God. So it's a good indicator of your natural passion. When you feel it the message is clear: you're close to your purpose.

If you live your passion, your vitality will naturally motivate you. Without passion your life will be driven by will-power alone. You'll know this if you usually have to drag yourself out of bed in the morning. So what does it for you? What really fires you up with enthusiasm? Make as long a list as you can.

ENTHUSIASM

_____

_____

_____

_____

_____

_____

_____

VALUES

Values are the guidelines by which we live. They are deeply rooted beliefs that powerfully influence us. Values are formed early in our lives and they function unconsciously, piloting our decisions and actions. They're so deeply rooted that we respond to them without even being aware of what's driving us. But we need to know consciously what they are because we only feel satisfied when our decisions are aligned to our deepest values. Only by understanding what they are can we get a grip on our behaviour. They give us the awareness to take charge of our lives.

Use the values table *below* to mark off ten of your most important values. This will enable you to analyse the priority values behind your decisions

Values table

Accommodating	❑	Elegance	❑
Acknowledgement	❑	Empathy	❑
Admiration	❑	Energetic	❑
Adventure	❑	Enthusiasm	❑
Aesthetics	❑	Environment	❑
Affection	❑	Ethics	❑
Agreeableness	❑	Excellence	❑
Ambition	❑	Excitement	❑
Arts	❑	Expertise	❑
Assertiveness	❑	Fame	❑
Attention to detail	❑	Family	❑
Balance	❑	Fast living	❑
Beauty	❑	Fearlessness	❑
Challenge	❑	Fighting spirit	❑
Change and variety	❑	Financial security	❑
Community	❑	Flexibility	❑
Competence	❑	Freedom	❑
Competitive	❑	Friendship	❑
Conservative	❑	Fulfilment	❑
Consistency	❑	Fun	❑
Co-operation	❑	Generosity	❑
Country (Pride)	❑	Gentleness	❑
Courage	❑	Goal orientated	❑
Creativity	❑	Goodness	❑
Decency	❑	Happiness	❑
Decisiveness	❑	Health	❑
Democracy	❑	Helpfulness	❑
Determination	❑	Honesty	❑
Effectiveness	❑	Honour	❑

Hopefulness	❏	Order	❏
Hospitality	❏	Passion	❏
Idealism	❏	Patience	❏
Inner harmony	❏	Peace	❏
Innocence	❏	Perfection	❏
Innovation	❏	Persistence	❏
Inquisitiveness	❏	Personal growth	❏
Integrity	❏	Persuasion	❏
Intellectual status	❏	Pleasure	❏
Intelligence	❏	Popularity	❏
Intimacy	❏	Positive	❏
Intuition	❏	Power	❏
Involvement	❏	Practical	❏
Job security	❏	Pressure (work)	❏
Joyfulness	❏	Pride	❏
Justice	❏	Privacy	❏
Knowledge	❏	Purity	❏
Leadership	❏	Quality	❏
Leisure time	❏	Questioning	❏
Liberalism	❏	Radical thinking	❏
Liveliness	❏	Rationality	❏
Love	❏	Realism	❏
Loyalty	❏	Relationships	❏
Materialism	❏	Relaxation	❏
Meaningful work	❏	Religion	❏
Merit	❏	Reputation	❏
Moderation	❏	Resourcefulness	❏
Money	❏	Respect	❏
Morality	❏	Responsibility	❏
Mystery	❏	Risk taking	❏
Nature	❏	Satisfaction	❏
Objectivity	❏	Self-esteem	❏
Openness	❏	Sensitivity	❏
Optimism	❏	Sensuality	❏

Sociability	❑	Tolerance	❑
Solitude	❑	Tradition	❑
Spirituality	❑	Truth	❑
Spontaneity	❑	Understanding	❑
Sport	❑	Unique	❑
Stability	❑	Wealth	❑
Status	❑	Wisdom	❑
Stimulation	❑	Worthiness	❑
Tenderness	❑	Youthfulness	❑

Once you've done this cross off five of the original ten that are less important to you. Remember that all ten are meaningful, but what we're aiming for are your priorities, the values that you'll be unable to compromise. Now you're left with five critical values. Next cross off the three of these that are less important than the others. This will leave you with two. Make a decision between the remaining two as to which is the priority value in your life right now. This is the value that guides much of your behaviour and it must be included somewhere in your mission statement. Either it must be contained in the wording or your mission must implicitly allow you to live accordingly.

This is significant because if your mission is at odds with your values, it'll be like wearing shoes one size too small. Every time you move you'll be reminded of the bad fit. The same applies to our relationships. Values cement our alliances and if you're in a relationship or work for a company whose values are at odds with your own, happiness will be difficult for you to maintain.

FUTURE PROJECTIONS

The present is filled with the counsel of the past and the sign-posts of the future. It's the starting point to make tomorrow's dreams a reality. Explore your dreams now by toying with the gift of your imagination. Take yourself on an imaginative adventure by visualising your life in ten or twenty years' time. Let your mind play with all sorts of possibilities.

Have fun with this because our imagination is not constrained by reality checks, so your mind will be free to explore all sorts of new ideas. At the same time keep in touch with your feelings. When you're through write down the ideas that excited you the most.

FUTURE DESIRES

_____

_____

_____

_____

_____

_____

_____

CREATING YOUR MISSION STATEMENT

To write your mission statement you'll need to review the work you've done so far. Use the steps below to summarise your personal exploration:

Step one – Self-analysis:

Which of your personal qualities are you most comfortable with (from page 116-117)?

_____

_____

_____

_____

_____

In a phrase can you summarise the interests, gifts and strengths you detailed on page 118?

Describe three things that are unique about you.

Step two – Enthusiasm
Write down the three things that you feel most enthusiastic about (from page 120).

Step three – Values
Write down your number one priority value.

Step four – Role models
What qualities in other people do you hold in high esteem?

Step five – Visualisation
Write a phrase describing what you desire in your future. Use the visualisation on page 124.

Step six – Regrets
Write down the regrets that you feel you may have in future that would concern you most.

_____

_____

_____

LOOK FOR TRENDS

Review the summary starting on page 124 and specifically look for similarities. These patterns are there for good reason. It's no coincidence that you've landed where you are today. Throughout your life your mind has guided your experiences to prepare you for your unique contribution. The trends that you see now alert you to the area where you can make a difference in future. If you're people orientated, you'll see this written all over the summary sheet. Likewise, those who have a technology bent will see this occurring repeatedly.

WRITING YOUR MISSION

To use your mission statement as the guideline for your life it'll need to be short. You simply won't remember a lengthy paragraph, so keep it down to a maximum of four or five words. The trends that you spotted in your summary sheet provide the starting point for you to play with some phrases. Use terms that are meaningful to you. No one else need understand them. This is your mission statement. Make sure that it excites and inspires you.

My personal mission statement:

_____

_____

Over the period of a few weeks apply your mission statement to your life and check whether it fits or not. Keep reviewing and changing it until it feels right. Once you've discovered it use it to test the decisions that you make about your life. Have it in mind always and keep reviewing your actions against it. Constantly check whether you're living on purpose.

If you really are at a loss, ask your subconscious mind for assistance. Remember that your mind knows what your life purpose is and the best time to access it is just prior to going to sleep. Every night ask the question and the message will come. It may be in a dream or via something someone else says; but if you're open to it, your mind will give you the information that you need.

Having a vision or mission is a basic plan of action that steers you in a chosen direction. But it will only serve you if you act. All that it reveals is a clear picture of our desired destination. So if you don't work out an itinerary, make the bookings and get yourself onto a flight, you'll join the ten per cent of dreamers who remain stuck in the mundane suburbia of their minds.

But when vision is backed by action it becomes the driving force in our lives. It gets us through difficult and trying times because even boring tasks become charged with purpose. This infuses our action with high levels of energy and our natural resources are drawn into the process. Vision also focuses our attention on making a difference. It prevents us from becoming scattered and wasting energy on meaningless activities. We can also use it to appraise our progress. Regular reviews motivate us to achieve bigger and better rewards. Emotionally intelligent people know that having a vision is a highly valuable life-skill. They use it constantly to keep making a difference. Discovering your purpose and living it is the greatest gift that you can give yourself.

Goal posts

Having established a clear vision or mission statement, you now know where your life is heading. But having a vision doesn't necessarily place you in the proactive camp – not yet anyway. To turn your vision into reality, you'll need to plan your growth and this is where goals come in. Goals keep challenges alive; and every time that you achieve something new you've satisfied your human need for growth, for more personal development. This is an insatiable need and just when you think that you've achieved your dreams there will be further challenges to face in the future. Recall that growth is an instinct and that each growth stage referred to in chapter 7 has different requirements. So even reaching wisdom is not a signal to relax the demands of your instincts.

This continual need to grow struck me some time ago after a friend of mine had achieved his most ambitious goal. His story is one that's so haunting I couldn't help but learn from it. It taught me that having only a single dream – even if it's a big one – isn't enough to fulfil this instinctive need. As such it also provides a clear indication of why striving for goals throughout our lives is critical to our well-being.

Tony was 23 when I met him and, being of a similar age myself, we were young and somewhat foolish. But Tony was different. He had set his mind on becoming a millionaire by age 30. At the time he was in the throes of developing a construction business; and like any new business it had more downs than ups during the difficult early days. This didn't put Tony off and week in and week out he pursued bigger and better contracts. By the time he was 29 he had reached his goal. Unlike the rest of us who were living from hand-to-mouth, Tony was buying expensive property, fancy cars, racehorses and negotiating a share of a large, luxurious seafaring yacht. He had it made and we admired him as a rebel who had taken on the establishment and won.

At the time Tony – like so many others – was also dabbling in drugs, but nobody thought much of it. At his numerous wild weekend parties he provided marijuana and cocaine as generously as other people offered a drink. It was only when he started on crack that eyebrows really lifted. By then it was already too late. Tony was a full-blown addict and what was left of his personality soon became intolerable. As he was unwilling to accept help, his friends began abandoning him. Inevitably his business also fell apart.

Tony was last seen in passing by a mutual friend. His sleek Mercedes Sports had been replaced by a battered wreck and his country mansion by a 'doss-house' room in the sleaziest part of town. Within just a few years, tycoon Tony reported that he had snorted the equivalent of $2 million. It was speculated that the only way that he could be maintaining his habit was as a pimp for the prostitutes that are so prevalent in the locality he now calls 'home'.

The fact that Tony is still alive is a miracle. But it must be remembered that he made his choices, so it's impossible for anyone else to judge his situation. Being ambitious myself, his experiences frightened me, so I needed to learn what could have happened to his raw aspirations in such a short time. He had a dream – one of the essential ingredients in success – and he fulfilled it at a young age. But having garnered wealth and the status of success, did he perhaps wonder what could be next? Was there anything that could possibly replace the adrenalin of becoming a multi-millionaire in just five short years? Perhaps he burnt out. Or was it that he had no further dream, nothing else to strive for?

GROWTH: A DEMANDING INSTINCT

If we examine his story in the context of personal growth, his situation is a powerful example of what can potentially happen if we stop channelling our energy into fulfilling our need for growth. For Tony, his escape was drugs. For many millions of others it's an addiction to boredom. Both are equally crippling, but stagnation just causes a slower more agonising death. Tony had the passion to fulfil his dream; and desire is certainly necessary, but unfortunately not sufficient to sustain success. Sustainable achievement means seeing the fulfilment of each of your goals as a stepping stone along the way. For long-term fulfilment, this process only stops with death.

In Tony's case it's also interesting that he was known for wanting things and wanting them now. This explains the rapid rise in his financial accomplishments; but this need for instant gratification could also have been his biggest downfall. It's the most likely reason for his addiction. One of the hallmarks of emotionally intelligent people is the ability to control their impulses. Impulses bombard us all the time; and whether it's a whim for a piece of chocolate or a new car, these flights of fancy can interfere with our ability to achieve more meaningful goals. They're distractions and it takes will-power to keep our impulses under control. This is what's meant by the ability to delay gratification and it's the mark of those with a healthy EQ.

THE MARSHMALLOW TEST

The earliest research into the field of EQ shows that children who are able to delay gratification are far more likely to succeed later in adult life. Daniel Goleman reports extensively in his book on the now-familiar 'marshmallow experiment'. Here four-and five-year-olds were given a couple of these tempting confections with one simple instruction: before they could devour them they were asked to wait five minutes for the experimenter to return from a pretend errand. If the children could wait, they were given double the number as a reward.

The results of this rather unassuming experiment were astonishing. As these small children grew up they were regularly observed. Consistently it was found that those who had waited scored significantly higher on their SAT scores and were more successful later in adult life. Boys who couldn't delay gratification were more likely to get involved in crime, gangs and drugs; and not surprisingly girls in this category often fell pregnant at an early age.

Now if you're a parent, before you decide that impulse control means depriving your children, read on. Children learn by example, so deprivation is only likely to make them swing the other way once they're free of your control. If you want to teach your children to delay gratification, you'll need to be an example of it yourself. Let them hear you discuss how you're going to wait until you can afford to build on that extra room or buy that new dining-room suite. Act accordingly and this will help them learn the skill far more profoundly than any form of deprivation.

The ability to delay gratification is vital to success because a lack of impulse control interferes with the process of reaching your goals. Think back to when you were studying. If you were like I was, it was so tempting to go to the movies, the pub, see a friend or do anything rather than pore over those dreadfully dull books.

But if you gave in to these distractions, it would have directly affected your grades. Now as an adult if you're living on credit it's an example of the same lack of control. In the university of life it too will impact on your results.

I WANT IT 'CAUSE I WANT IT

Yet our world is geared towards instantly gratifying our whims. We have instant coffee, instant fun and worse still advertising constantly bombards our impulses. It taps directly into our need for immediate gratification and whatever's being sold we want now, now, NOW! This can get us into an endless cycle of debt; and while we're overwhelmed by how much we owe, it's hard to focus on what we want to achieve in future. This is how our need for instant gratification interferes with our ability to achieve more meaningful life-goals.

The need for instant gratification has become a modern drug. It's as addictive as cocaine. Just look at the success of infomercials. Many people can't help but pick up the phone and get themselves a 'gift' through the mail. My husband and I witnessed this when we were looking to buy a new house. At the time those fancy walking machines were being marketed heavily. During our search for a new abode we must have seen dozens of them – they made very convenient clotheshorses. It's a strange phenomenon in our society: just paying the money for the machine is as good as getting the exercise job done. It's what we hope for with instant gratification.

While buying a walker may not set you back too badly, a general lack of impulse control will. Someone I once knew was such an extreme example of the inability to delay gratification that her story is almost hard to believe.

She was heavily overweight. So much so that she battled to walk. This was not a result of genetics but simply from gluttony. To support her elaborate lifestyle she was also deeply in debt. Even so she claimed to be proud of being what she called an 'instant grat-cat'. To get rid of the financial heavies she simply borrowed more, usually from her friends. This meant that her friendships tended to be short-lived and she had to keep finding new stock regularly – preferably those who could provide more money.

To justify her behaviour she had apparently turned to spiritual principles, which she used to defend her actions. She ultimately used them to con other people. This particular incident was for a so-called 'investment' in a spiritual exercise 'guaranteed' to pay thousands. However, it was subsequently discovered that the money was used for an exotic trip from which the grat-cat had not returned. But things started to fall into place when this woman's landlord told me he'd learnt just how much money the grat-cat owed. The last I heard, she'd been jailed on fraud charges. Clearly the situation had got completely out of control.

The tragedy is that this grat-cat had a real need to make a difference. But her lack of impulse control clouded her views. It kept her in a state of such financial anxiety that she had difficulty focusing on more constructive longer-term goals.

Now this is not to say that you need live like a pauper. Not at all. In life you can have whatever you want, but there are always consequences to your actions. If these don't harm you or those around you, then it's not an issue of instant gratification. But if your desires put you into severe debt, create havoc in your relationships or interfere with your achievements then you are caught in this endless cycle. We all want stuff and want it now, but those with a healthy level of EQ know that their well-being is not dependent on acquiring these things.

CREDIT YOURSELF

Examine now what your tempting marshmallows could be. Where do you find it difficult to control your impulses? If you're in debt, it could be an insatiable desire for material goods like gadgets, CDs, clothing, jewellery, new appliances or other luxury items. Or if you're overweight, is your indulgence in the food line? For some it's about attention. This is true if you inappropriately demand acknowledgement, recognition or need to be centre-stage in every situation. This will reveal itself as difficulties in your relationships. For others it's about sex, gambling, alcohol or drugs – even the pills you get on prescription. Whatever your marshmallows may be, identify them now by writing them down.

Obviously if you're suffering from debilitating addictions, you'll need to get help with impulse control. Find it through joining Alcoholics Anonymous or any of the similar agencies dealing with gambling, drugs and sex addictions. But mostly people struggle against their need for instant gratification in other areas. If yours fall into the more 'innocent' categories, turn these into rewards for completing a job well done. Instead of buying these items on your credit card set up a credit facility with yourself. For instance tell yourself that you can have those desirable items only once you've got the deal that you've been working on. When the deal goes through it's such a good feeling to reward yourself – especially because your achievements mostly make it possible for you to afford what you want.

I was talking to a friend who has almost everything; and instead of buying more goods he likes to reward himself with the best champagne and a generous quantity of smoked salmon. For him this is sheer bliss. It's also a terrific way to celebrate success because it involves taking the time to recognise and acknowledge yourself. My own reward is unusual jewellery. Previously my desires would get me into debt; now I buy pieces to venerate my achievements. Every time I wear them I remember the success each particular item represents. It's much more satisfying than being reminded of the financial liability jewellery used to cause me.

GOAL ORIENTED

Having a line of credit with yourself also keeps you focused on your goals or next desirable achievement. Although much has been written and said about the importance of goals, it's unusual to find people who know what they want. Over the years I have trained thousands of people and if there have been two who had a clear idea of where their lives were heading, it's a lot. Interestingly, I would readily categorise both as proactive people. Without a doubt they could be grouped in the ten per cent discussed in chapter 8. So what about the rest, the 90 per cent who have little idea about where their life is heading? If you're one of them – and I hope you're not – it's likely that other people have taken control of your destiny. Remember that if you aren't in control of your life, someone else will be for sure. Is this what you want?

In this ever-changing world goals are vital. With so many distractions it's easy to let the years go by without achieving the things that you want. Think about it. Over the last five years how many of your personal desires have you fulfilled? Are you where you expected to be at this stage in your life? If not, it's probably because of a lack of direction. Indeed things change, but if your goals are important you need to keep yourself on track. Goals are like a road map, and even if we take a few unexpected turns we still need to have a clear idea of where we're heading.

I saw the power of goals when one of my brothers decided to move city. He's a brilliant interior designer and had bought a charming house to renovate – for charming read 'broken'.

Over the four years he owned it this was a work in progress – one that seemed to make little headway over time. He always had other business commitments and eventually we rather unkindly gave it an appropriate name – 'little Bosnia'. However, once he made a decision to move, things started to change rapidly.

Within two months Bosnia was transformed into its promised charm and when selling it he got a whopping great price. Goals focus our attention; and instead of allowing distractions or excuses to side-track us, we find purpose in getting on with the job.

I've found this to be most beneficial in my fitness regime. I maintain a reasonably regular schedule, but often find the couch-potato routine more appealing. However, once I started entering marathon cycle races, my attention was focused on completing these punishing events. Now, even when I'm not in the mood for exercise, I just have to think about an unfit struggle up those wretched hills and the bum gets right onto that bicycle. So wherever you're finding it hard to focus, set yourself some goals – ones that you're prepared to commit to.

To be meaningful, goals need to contribute to your mission and, yes, even fitness does this. The benefits of accomplishing your aims must also excite you. Anyone in sales will tell you that you can't sell anything to anyone if you don't inspire them with benefits.

The same applies to goals. Sell the benefits of achieving your goals to yourself. How will you feel when XYZ is done? What will you gain as a result? This excitement will keep your energy flowing. It's the power that motivates you to achieve more in future.

It's a question of time

Also don't put yourself under too much pressure. Set goals that are challenging but attainable. People often get themselves into trouble because they overestimate the time available. If you are prone to this, go easy on yourself. If you don't, you'll end up dissatisfied with your efforts every year. This will only make you despondent and set up a cycle where you're constantly berating yourself.

Time is an issue because it's fixed and immoveable. We only have so much of it and this is where we need to be realistic. Dream big dreams but be pragmatic in your planning. The one thing that we tend to forget is that you can always bank on other people making demands on you. More often than not their needs will interfere with your goals, so cater for this by building in a degree of flexibility. You may need to rearrange your process to meet some unexpected future demands.

STARVE THE ENEMY

During my seminars I conduct an exercise about goals. It's a simple one and it involves connecting consecutive numbers on a page. To begin with delegates are asked to reach the highest number they can in a timed minute. When they begin they're quite relaxed. For round two I then ask them to set a goal by identifying the number that they would like to achieve during the next round. Every time I do this the atmosphere shifts. Faces grimace as they tense up and many are not beyond swearing at themselves out loud. Usually they do a lot worse than in the previous round. If this is you under pressure, remember that lambasting yourself only feeds the enemy within. While it's active, you'll find any new challenges difficult to overcome.

ENJOY THE RIDE

Another pitfall is that so many people fail to make their goals fun. You simply aren't going to be motivated by a goal that demands cleaning the kitchen floor every day. Use your goals to break new ground and the excitement will come from gaining more confidence through self-discovery. Keep focused on finding out more about who you are and the process of achieving your goals will become an exploratory adventure. Self-discovery happens through all manner of exciting activities. Make sure that these are built into your process.

While breaking new ground understand that in one way or another we're all a bit scared of the unknown. Don't expect to cope initially and be kind to yourself when you're floundering. From previous chapters we know that our most powerful learning happens on the path to mastery. This is the source of personal satisfaction and understanding it is critical to savouring your successes. Always remember to enjoy the journey. It prevents the victory from being hollow when it eventually comes.

With these issues in mind, start considering your goals for the next year and once you've done so write them down. This is the start of the plan to give your life direction. Make sure you've written them because if they're just floating in your head, you'll lose sight of them when the next crisis comes around. Remember to be realistic about time, so only set two or three major goals for the year. Next put in deadlines and write these into your diary. Diarise the start date, reminders to yourself and your completion deadline. Then peg some of your personal marshmallows as rewards for each level of achievement. Use this example as a guideline:

	Deadlines	
Goals for the year	**Start**	**Completion**

Reward	**Benefits**

Although not so long ago people set fixed five- and ten-year plans, with the increasing pace of change it's now unrealistic to do so. Change brings many new possibilities and rigidly sticking to a ten-year plan could mean missing some valuable opportunities along the way. Rather see your plan to fulfil your mission more like a spider's web than a path. Your mission provides an overall direction, but there's no single track to reach it. Each compartment in the web contains critical steps to achieving your mission; and you'll need to consider these now.

DESIGN YOUR LIFE

Using the spider's web diagram as a guideline, design these future steps before you continue. Fill in the challenges you'll need to meet to achieve your life purpose. This may be a five- or fifteen-year web, but design it to suit your needs. In the example given you'll notice that some years have four goals and others only two. This depends on the magnitude of the goals that you set. Custom design your own to suit your mission or purpose.

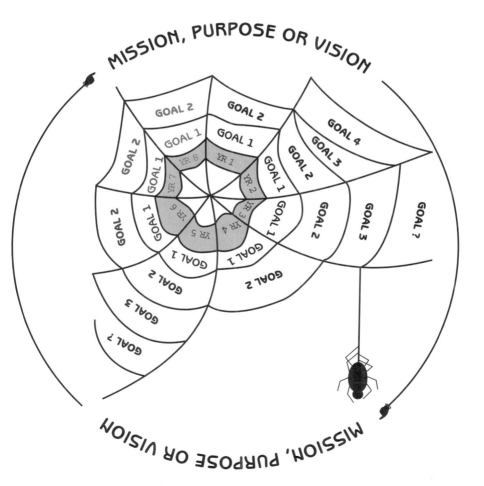

The purpose of the web is to cater for change. For example, as you progress you may find that an opportunity presents itself now to fulfil a year-four goal. Be flexible. If this happens, rearrange and adapt your web to suit your changing circumstances. Pull this goal out of year four and include it in this year's plan. It may mean rescheduling some of your current annual goals to cater for time limitations. But no matter how much rearranging your web requires, be committed to the process. This will necessitate dropping some of the excuses you make to yourself for non-performance.

Don't read on until you have completed this section. If you haven't written your goals, consider whether this corresponds with any feelings of dissatisfaction you may have. This will continue until you clearly define the direction that you want your life to take and start getting active.

Also, unlike Tony, once you've achieved these goals you must keep expanding on them. Specific longer-term goals that don't fit your current web may be difficult to pinpoint accurately now. But the closer you get to fulfilling this plan, the more you'll need to keep thinking about your goals. Keep yourself on course by continually questioning where your life is heading. Always remember that the decisions you make today dictate your life tomorrow.

THE BIG 'C' WORD

Keeping yourself on track also means being committed to creating the life you want. While commitment may seem like a word with heavy connotations it's really quite a simple concept. John-Roger and Peter McWilliams suggest that it's a triangle involving your thoughts, feelings and actions. If all three are involved in designing your life then you are committed. It's about being stimulated to achieve your goals, feeling excited about the benefits and taking action. But if one of the three aspects is missing the consequences are fairly predictable.

If you think that your goals are a good idea and feel excited about them but fail to act, expect to experience something similar to getting your car stuck in sand. Excitement releases energy so your engine is revving; but the wheels just spin making it impossible for you to move forward. It's frustrating and the frustration is a message telling you to move on, to get active. Start by breaking your goals down into manageable steps. Begin by setting a deadline to implement the very first stage of step one. Even if it's as small as making a phone call or getting some information, action will commit you to your new ideas. This will relieve the frustration.

If, on the other hand, you think that your goals are a good idea and act without feeling excited about them, persistence will be a problem. Often, men socialised into traditional roles fall into this trap. For men the goal in business is more about producing wealth than life-fulfilment. But if your heart's not in what you're doing, it's hard to stay committed during tough times. Check whether your mission excites you. Does it have roots in your enthusiasm? If not, go back to the analysis in chapter 8 and review where your heart really lies.

The last corner of the triangle deals with not thinking things through. You feel like something and do it and this can lead to addictions. Sometimes people are hooked on improvement kicks; but often this lack of commitment is about succumbing to addictive depressions, boredom or stagnation. Addictions can be broken by continually questioning your actions. Ask yourself the question from chapter 4, 'Why do I make the choices I do?' Don't stop questioning until you come up with some real answers. No one can change your addictions except you: and this kind of questioning will provide you with some valuable clues.

Your life is in your hands and even if your guidance is spiritual, the way that you shape and form your reality is still up to you. Your existence is created by the choices you make; and the

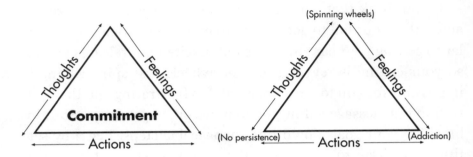

more that you can accurately plan your passage, the easier it'll be to navigate through life's obstacles. Goals aren't just 'nice-to-haves': they're essential to your growth, and the strange thing is the more you grow, the better your shot at success. Don't let the years roll by without having firm goals to work on. Many people do this and they end up bitter and frustrated about what life failed to dish out to them. Avoid being one of them and the best precaution you can take is to regain control of your life. Being 'response-able', directed and committed makes you ready to roll out the most enrapturing reality imaginable. Entertain it, act on it and, I guarantee you, you'll attain it.

Relax or relapse

For years managing stress has been a hot item on many people's personal agendas. Yet it often remains something to address in future ... after all, we're far too busy to look at it now! Since the eighties much has been written about stress; and although we presently have a wealth of information, we still live highly stressed lives. We know that it manifests as a common cause of many life-threatening illnesses. Even so, many people find it hard to address this familiar ailment because it's a difficult one to understand. Stress does, however, start to make sense when we review it in terms of energy. So without spending too much time covering old ground, we'll begin by uncovering the emotional basis for stress.

From the existing body of literature we know that two forms of stress exist – good stress and bad stress. We also know that without the healthy form of stress it would be difficult to get out of bed in the morning. We just couldn't get ourselves going. This corresponds with the two forms of motivation discussed in chapter 3. Good stress exists when we're motivated to achieve the things that we want. Bad stress comes into the picture when we're fighting against whatever we don't accept in our lives. The second form is what we mean when we say that we're stressed.

Good stress is stored energy; and using it to achieve what you want means consuming it productively. Bad stress is energy stored in the mental and emotional components. It drains into the areas you're stressing over and if it's not used to take action it continues to dam up. It's a bit like stagnant water. If it doesn't flow it begins to get contaminated. So being anxious about things that don't suit you just causes more and more energy to build up in these areas. Eventually the dam wall bursts and this unhealthy energy causes an explosion. Stressed people have a short fuse, but each eruption causes a big energy loss. It leaves little power to manage the crisis or solve the problem. This endless cycle just adds more stress to an already overburdened system.

As an exercise, write down what's causing stress in your life currently. Don't just think about it, it will only become real for you if you write it down. Don't read on until you've got a handle on the stressors in your life. Now give each item a tick depending on whether it's something you are striving for or a cross if it's something you're fighting against.

If the majority of items on your list are crosses, you're fighting an uphill battle against life. Now examine these items. Which of them can you personally address and what can you do to change them? If you're unsure, read on. But if you haven't completed this exercise yet, question whether you're really committed to managing your stress, or are you just kidding yourself?

Remember from chapter 1 that your energy or life-force can be drained by choices you've made or things that you've allowed to happen to you. So if the pot's dry, you'll be left to manage your life through will-power alone. This is stressful because to survive you're having to push uphill without the support of your major resource – your energy.

Stress, like everything else, boils down to the choices we make; and if we're feeling stressed it's because we are mismanaging our options. Managing stress involves self-control; and to deal appropriately with your stress you'll need to consider how you govern your choices. By now many of the choices you've made have probably become firmly entrenched habits. These habitual responses need to be reviewed in four energy areas: your physical, emotional, mental and spiritual practices.

PHYSICAL

This area has been covered extensively in the stress literature. Yet if you still eat badly, don't get enough sleep, are unfit, have a number of addictions and have little time for relaxation, expect to be stressed. Recall from chapter 1 that these are the areas that are draining your energy. If the plug is pulled because of your poor physical habits, what do you have left to manage the other three areas?

Your physical body is the vehicle that carries the rest of you around. If you're ignoring the fact that it badly needs a service, you're heading for a breakdown. For me this was and still is my biggest challenging area. For many years I just expected my body to cope and only after being hospitalised did the message eventually sink in. But instead of attempting to change all of my bad habits at once (because I'd been this route before and failed), I've found far greater success from addressing one area at a time. First I reviewed my diet. Previously addicted to rich food – usually of the junk variety – I now find that if I don't eat something fresh regularly I start to crave it. It's a sign that the new habit is clicking in.

Then I looked at exercise. I was a great one for signing up long-term contracts at health clubs and only going for a few months. Only once I found a form of exercise that I really enjoyed was I able to sustain it. Now that I'm fit it's easy to maintain. Exercise also has the additional benefit of making me want to drink lots of water, a taste I had particular difficulty acquiring. So if gym isn't for you, try walking, rebounding, swimming, spinning, Tai Chi or playing tennis; but whatever exercise you do make sure that it's enjoyable. After a while you'll find that if you miss a week or two your body will start demanding it. It's just a question of the habit you're in.

When it comes to rest and relaxation (R&R), I had to learn to be more disciplined. Now I take lots of holidays, have a weekly massage, a monthly facial, take time off and am learning to read novels rather than always studying non-fiction. In a hectic world, relaxation is absolutely essential if you want to be productive. It was hard for me to accept this: but our minds simply cannot operate at full tilt twenty-four hours a day. However, I learnt that if I wasn't taking enough time off I was just forcing a situation where I had to work harder and longer just to get by.

People who work smart know the importance of R & R. They understand that good ideas mainly come from a more relaxed mind and they take time off to generate them. Think about your habits and how much time you give yourself. What needs to change and what are you going to do about it?

For me these new habits have taken a couple of years to entrench. Even so, there are still a number of health items on my agenda. These too will be addressed in the future. But the point is, take your physical needs one at a time. If you attempt simultaneously to change your diet, start an exercise regime, give up all your addictions and introduce disciplined relaxation time, you're setting yourself up for failure. Your system can't handle this much change all at once and you'll probably soon start rebelling against your own demands. Give yourself a break! Instead set up a step-by-step plan for change. Prioritise your physical needs and introduce this plan into your goal strategy developed in the previous chapter.

EMOTIONAL

Emotional stress exists because we've invested too much power in a relationship, our career or even our fears; and this controls us. These are the areas our energy is damming up. From chapter 2 we learnt to manage our emotions as messages and to distinguish between anxiety and motivation. Also, from chapter 3 we learnt to choose our responses. These new habits will teach you to become more emotionally robust and this will alleviate the stress that results from not being in control of your life. What remains to be addressed are the environmental stressors, the external issues that we feel so strongly about.

Environmental stress is about pushing uphill. Things that you feel you can do little to address are consuming your energy. In some of my seminars I ask delegates to specify what makes them stressed and many write lengthy lists about the state of the government, crime, taxes and their children's safety or education. But the question is: what are we going to do about it? We all know that if someone cuts us off in the traffic there's no point in getting uptight. Of course this is a bland example when compared to the real stressors we face. But the point is that if we can't do anything to address these issues then our agitation is as futile as getting upset with other road-users.

Rising fear won't help us to manage our emotional stress level. It will only make it more unmanageable. It happens when we confuse environmental stress with concern. If we were concerned enough, we'd tap into our resources and address these real social problems. The fact that many people don't means it's easier to allow our fear-based stress to immobilise us. Then we use our apathy as a convenient excuse to do nothing. We even say, 'Well what can one person do anyway?' Each of us can do a lot when we stop confusing stress with concern.

If it's stress, deal with your fears and accept that you aren't going to do anything about the problem. This is far healthier than constantly banging on about what other people should be doing to address the issues you're worrying about. Remember from your emotional messages that worry masks your personal fears. Instead of projecting these onto the external environment, address these fears and then review what's left of your environmental concerns.

To many of you this probably sounds a bit harsh. But consider it again. If you aren't prepared to address your worries through action then why carry around this burdensome excess baggage? If it's your children you're worried about, think how your stress is affecting them. Is your anxiety about their future adding anything to their lives? I doubt it.

If on the other hand it's real concern then the tension you feel is telling you to do something about it. It's providing you with the energy necessary to act. Offer to help, pay or even do something as easy as writing to your local authority. But be more proactive than just complaining. Gather people together and come up with real workable solutions. Proposing solutions will guarantee your letter more of a hearing than those who are simply grousing.

The same applies to issues in the work environment. Whenever I conduct business seminars, I advise staff who are experiencing problems to stop dumping their stuff on management. Whether you like it or not, managers are unlikely to do much about your problems because they have their own issues and priorities to consider. For your own sanity rather be proactive. Take initiative. Develop what Stephen Covey calls 'win-win' solutions and implement them. Once you demonstrate how everyone will benefit from your solution, it's much more likely to gain acceptance. On the other hand, if your solution is inappropriate, you'll soon know all about it. Sure you may have to take some flak, but this kind of opposition is easier to handle than the longer-term frustration of damming up your own energy.

I saw a wonderful example of this in South Africa just after the transition to democracy. For most parents in this country education is a major concern, but particularly for people who were previously disadvantaged by the old South African apartheid system. Left without resources and funds, the likelihood of underprivileged children becoming educated in the short term was minimal. This didn't, however, deter a few powerful spirits in one of the country's poorest areas. Here a group of pioneering parents got together and pooled their resources. Although money was tight some could produce bricks and others could lay them. A few were carpenters, some were cabinetmakers and others were seamstresses. Together these extraordinarily committed people built a school in their area. Today it's the pride of their community.

Now, parents who earn pay the teacher's salaries and those who don't offer their services. This means that pupils not only learn to read and write, but they're also getting lessons in various trades. This will benefit them greatly in future. Stories like this and others, such as Oprah Winfrey's *Angel Houses* (funded but built by local communities), are heart-warming evidence that people can constructively use their pent-up energy. It's so much healthier than sitting around becoming more and more incensed by one's own complaining.

Therefore, instead of carrying environmental stress around, make a choice about the socio-economic burdens for which you're going to take responsibility. Only choose those to which you're willing and able to respond. Do whatever you can in this area and encourage others – particularly if they complain – to get active about their own social baggage. Yes we can each make a difference; and if all of us contributed to our area of passion, many of the environmental stressors we experience would be alleviated. But it's up to no one else but ourselves.

MENTAL

Mental stress arises from making some things too important and this causes our energy or power to be wrapped up in these areas. If for example your ego – or sense of self-importance – is out of control then much of your energy will be trapped in projecting the image that fits your perceived status. Having the right car, house or social engagements will be what controls you and any threat to your position is likely to be a major source of stress.

This happens when your head rules your life rather than your heart.

Whether it's your status, the IRS, an exam or a project deadline, all mental stressors need to be put into perspective. How important are these things in the bigger picture of your life? To get a grip on this it's easiest to turn to nature. If you can't take yourself to experience the magnificence of the mountains or the power of the ocean, go to a park or just look up at the stars. Consider your problem or issue in relation to the vast expanse in front of you and see it for what it really is. Is it so important that it warrants you being consumed by it?

Mental stressors, like money, have grown so out of proportion that we're living in a society prepared to kill for them. It's known that family murders are a South African phenomenon; and research into these great human tragedies usually turns up severe financial troubles as one of the major causes. Often fathers (but sometimes also mothers) who cannot see their way through the piling debts are driven to suicide – but they take their spouse and children with them. Sure it's hard to live without cash. But it also means that money is viewed so out of perspective in our world that it drives people to this level of desperation. Terrible tragedies like this happen when mental stress gets way out of proportion.

Although these are of course exceptional cases, they are the extreme result of too much mental pressure. This in turn has a deep impact on how we feel about ourselves; and the more insecure we become, the less we're able to tap the resources we need to address the problem. If you ever feel yourself sliding into desperation, stop and address the issues. If it's debt that's causing you such mental anguish, write down the full extent of it. Facing up to it will be the last thing you'll feel like doing, but you will feel better once you've clarified the picture. From past experience I can tell you it's a great relief. Then make a plan to pay off each person – even if it's a small amount – and keep in contact with them. Creditors would rather support you paying off debt than have you go into liquidation. For them, your going under means that they're likely to lose everything. Manage your fears this way rather than allowing your personal insecurities to sink you into hopelessness and desperation.

Another issue stemming from insecurity is the need for perfection. It's particularly prevalent in women and never before have I known a mental condition to be the source of such major stress. I was talking to a client who explained just how detrimental this need is in her life. 'I can't leave home in the morning until I've done certain things,' she said, 'but doing them the way I want them done usually makes me run late. And I can't stand being late so I tear through the traffic – getting more and more agitated – and by the time I get into the office I'm already a nervous wreck. Then if I have a meeting, which I usually do, I can't concentrate properly because I'm already in a state. Plus I'm also worried about whether the instructions I've rushed past my secretary will be complied with to my liking. Of course after the meeting I've had so much else on my mind that it's difficult to remember what was decided, so I have to go back and find out … and it's really embarrassing to appear so unprofessional.' And all this before tea-time! One can't even imagine what the rest of the day and the next and the next must be like.

The need for perfection is a peculiarity of Western society and it affects every area of life. Those who suffer from it believe that when their spouses don't behave or dress perfectly they're humiliated and when their children act like kids they're ashamed. So taking life personally forces them to control other people. As we know from an earlier chapter, this leaks emotional energy. Then with their energy being depleted by this irrational need they generally have little left to control themselves. Usually their own lives are a mess of crisis management. This they then use as ammunition to lambast themselves some more, which further damages their self-esteem. Yet ironically a poor self-image is what caused the need for perfection in the first place.

If you suffer from this malady for perfection, pull back the reins and take control of yourself. This will mean waging a war against the enemy within. Here the enemy is particularly cruel because it demands perfection and then laughs when it's made impossible. Constantly question your priorities and decide whether making the beds is more critical than your meeting. Put your energies into the events that are important and make it a rule to control only yourself. This means that if your husband leaves the house sporting a pink spotty tie on a lime-green shirt, bite your tongue – it's his responsibility! Also question when you will be satisfied that everything is perfect, including yourself. What measure do you have for this? How will you know when you've arrived at perfection? Or are you just going to continue trying to achieve the impossible?

Another attempt at the impossible, which is a major mental stressor, is having to make more time. In an earlier chapter we discussed that the problem isn't time, but how you manage your choices. There's a terrific training exercise that makes this point quite clearly.

If you had $86 400 put into your bank account every day how would you spend it? Would you save or invest some of it, spend it on a great holiday, buy stuff for others or get those things you've really been wanting? Well the same applies to time. Every day you have 86 400 seconds to live. How are you choosing to spend your time?

All forms of mental stress – including time – need a plan to address them. This means setting goals and sticking to your guns. If the goal is about making more time for yourself, leave the house in disarray until someone else takes responsibility for it. No matter how out of control the problem seems, you always have choices about it. Examine all possibilities and take cognisance of the habits that got you into a mess originally. Once you've learnt from these old bad habits you won't have to repeat them in future.

SPIRITUAL

Spiritual stress occurs when we're in the wrong career or job or don't feel that our lives are making a difference. The discipline of psychology refers to spiritual stress as an existential crisis – a crisis of being. It refers to how much meaning exists in your life. The more meaningful your existence, the less likely you are to experience this spiritual crisis. Many people find meaning and solace in either religion or spiritual practices; but if neither is for you, your human spiritual need is not an area to be ignored.

The older you are the more pronounced this need becomes; and feeling that life is empty is one of the main symptoms of spiritual stress. The emptiness feels acutely real because unless you're channelling your personal power into creating your life, your energy is being dispersed and wasted. This means that you're oozing power from your central source and little or nothing is left to feed the other areas. It's why spiritual stress is often experienced as depression.

People who invest much of their personal power in superficial matters like status and image are often hardest hit by this crisis. So too are women, but for different reasons. Women who've lived traditional lives as wives and mothers invest their power in their children. But once the children leave home, mothers often feel that their role has ended. This is commonly known as the 'empty-nest' syndrome because in the absence of the children life is perceived to have little value. Older women who overcome this find other outlets to channel their energy into and these become powerful new opportunities for growth.

I'll say it again ... recall that life at its essence is about growth. It means learning as much as you can from everything that happens to you. At no time can anyone afford to say, 'Well, I know all I need to know', because from that moment on the crisis of spirit will start killing you slowly. Every day is an opportunity for growth; and the more you grow, the more rewarding life becomes.

Chapter 8 deals with making a difference; and if you're still unsure about where you want to add value, keep working on your personal mission statement until you have a clear idea of your own direction. Don't be frightened of making changes. You are strong enough and if they're carefully planned you can even build in a safety net for your own security. Rely on your wealth of personal resources and ask if you need others to help you. Also remember that you're changing all the time. If you don't believe this think about who you were five or even ten years ago. I would hope that growth has fundamentally changed who you are today.

Part of this need for growth is retrieving lost energy and, spiritually, this means being able to forgive. Other people were only part of a bigger experience and you participated in it to learn something. So, if you've already learnt from the experience, there's no point in resenting them because it will feed them your most precious resource – your energy. Of course when we feel wronged, forgiveness is difficult. But would you rather endure the stress of continually investing power in the past or containing your energy to re-create a more exciting future? Learn, learn and learn from your experiences and you'll be able to forgive – both yourself and other people.

Related to forgiveness is the spiritual stress that arises from confrontations with our integrity. Integrity is your personal morality and it relates to your true values. Not living according to your priority values sets up a tension in your system. It's like an elastic band that pulls your actions back until your behaviour is more in line with your values. Every one of us has a shadow or dark side and what this means is that we're all capable of atrocities like violence, cheating, lying or many forms of debauchery. Except in extraordinary circumstances –

like a psychopathic personality – our conscience keeps us within our own integrity. It does so by creating stress when we're out of line. This discomfort exists so that we question our behaviour, learn from it and don't need to keep repeating painful experiences in future.

WILL-POWER

You'll recall from chapter 1 that our energy is contained by will-power; and for many people who've struggled to develop will it's not as hard as it sounds. If you've grappled in the past, it's only because your will-power wasn't backed by energy. This means that your intentions need to be fired by the energy of want and desire. Telling yourself you 'should', 'ought to' or 'must' do something is unlikely to sustain your commitment for long.

From the previous chapter you'll remember that real commitment requires us to think something is a good idea, to want to achieve it and to act upon it. Commitment brings together all the elements that make applying will-power far easier than having to battle constantly with ourselves. Battling causes enormous stress in our system; and if you're currently wrestling with an area in your life, look at which of the three essential components is missing.

Will-power is necessary to change old habits. You only got into these patterns by repeating the same behaviour over and over. So much so that you now believe it's part of who you are. But it's not. It's just behaviour you've learnt and any habit can be changed. The key to change lies in an old joke about how many psychiatrists it takes to change a light bulb. Only one ... but the light bulb must really want to change! If you don't truly want to change your habits then stop kidding yourself. It just wastes energy and time. But if you do, there's no hidden secret in developing your will. It's just a matter of consciously getting into new or different ways of living.

Think about it like going to the gym. When you start it's hard work. Just to get there you'll probably have to force yourself. Initially you'll sweat through it and it's likely to hurt. Every new stage will be an effort. To sustain it, it'll be a battle between your thoughts – wondering why you're doing this to yourself – and your desire to be fit. But if you keep a picture of a fitter and healthier you in your mind, you can overcome this kind of negativity. Once you start becoming fitter it will take less and less effort and, as I said earlier, you'll soon feel uncomfortable if you miss a few days. This means that the new habit is becoming part of you and once this happens it's so much easier to maintain.

The same applies to a new diet, curing an addiction, calming your fiery temper or dealing with your unreasonable need for perfection. Any one of these takes being aware of your old habit. Every time it rears its head, you'll need to apply will-power to behave differently. Like the gym, forcing your will upon the situation is only necessary in the beginning. All habits are self-sustaining, but they take lots of practice to acquire – even the bad ones. I remember when as a teenager I started smoking cigarettes. I coughed, got violently ill and didn't even particularly like it, but perseverance eventually won!

To reverse your stressful habits, take each one a step at a time. Some will impact on other habits (like drinking more water because you're exercising) and these are the only ones it's advisable to combine. Use the schedule *below* to help you plan your programme and add each stage to your goal strategy.

Physical:

Activity	Goal Date
_____	_____
_____	_____
_____	_____

Mental:

Activity   **Goal Date**

_____   _____

_____   _____

_____   _____

Emotional:

Activity   **Goal Date**

_____   _____

_____   _____

_____   _____

Spiritual:

Activity   **Goal Date**

_____   _____

_____   _____

_____   _____

Once you start making different choices your stress will become much more manageable. This isn't to say that you'll never experience stress again. You will, but you'll know how to manage it better. Remember to work with these four areas as a system; and if you know that you're entering a busy phase, be sure to step up your de-stressing activities in other areas. For example, if your stress level always rises during exams or at financial year-end, improve your diet, get enough sleep and avoid arguments in your relationships during this period. By looking after yourself in the areas other than the one causing your stress, you'll be able to keep yourself relatively balanced during these difficult times. Remember that EQ is about maintaining a sense of happiness. So addressing your stressors is a major step in creating a new happier, healthier and more relaxed you in future.

The love
that blinds

At this late stage in the book it seems a little ridiculous to say that none of the preceding chapters would matter if we could survive without other people. But by nature we're social and having relationships is one of our most central needs. People are business, people are fun and people are life. But what's important is that the quality of our relationships is only as good as our ability to manage ourselves. It's dependent on our level of self-control. So it's in this area that a healthy EQ really counts. Everything we've learnt so far is applied in our relationships. This is done with the aim of getting other people to co-operate with our plans. Remember that no one can succeed on their own and a high level of EQ helps us to make things happen.

Relationships are vital because it's only by experiencing ourselves in relation to others that we learn who we are. By evaluating our similarities and differences we begin to understand the multiple elements of our personality. Think about it for a minute. How would we know how intelligent, warm, sensitive and funny we are if it weren't for feedback from others? Just by being with other people we have a gauge of where we stand. So finding out who we are is one of the reasons that relationships are essential to our happiness as human beings.

Enjoying a close relationship is one of the most satisfying experiences we can encounter. It fulfils a vital human need and provides us with a safe emotional context to explore more of ourselves. Having strong alliances is something we all want because experiencing a real affiliation with another fulfils a deep yearning to belong. Yet, as wonderful as close relationships are, it's sad that so few people truly experience them. This is what we'll explore in this chapter. But before continuing, it must be said that the topic of relationships warrants volumes in itself. However, within the context of this work we will only explore the main themes.

RED HEARTS AND ROSES
One of the prime reasons for the lack of closeness in relationships is the way we choose partners. Do you remember when you last fell in love? Do you recall how that person sent your heart racing? How the 'will they call, kiss or bed me?' anticipation nearly drove you to distraction. And those long intense conversations where you were so locked into one another that nothing else seemed to matter. Also remember those explosive feelings: the ones that tickled your senses and made you feel alive, more alive than you've ever felt before. But as delightful as these sensations may be, the bubble is burst when we realise that this is neither love nor chemistry. Rather it's the deception of romance.

Romantic love drives our desires and although there can be no greater fleeting excitement, it's seldom the basis for a healthy close relationship. To explain I'll extrapolate from Robert Johnson's work, *The Psychology of Romantic Love*. Using the mythological tale of Tristan and Isolde, he explains that by the time we're young adults we already have a pretty firm idea of Mr or Ms Right. This notion is what we go seeking, often desperately.

When we meet someone who fits the part – even loosely – we start projecting our ideal picture onto them. Just by being there they provide a screen for our movie – *Perfect Partner* – and we fall hopelessly in love with the fantasy in our mind. Romantic love blinds us and we don't even see the person behind the screen. But, when we boil it down, what we've fallen in love with is the fabrication created by the rose-tinted spectacles of our desire.

Scott Peck in *The Road Less Travelled* estimates that our movie can have a successful run for about two years. During this exciting phase many tie the knot and only afterwards realise that things are different from what they imagined. You even hear people say, 'You're not the person I married' – and of course they're not because the screen has started to tear. Once the real person emerges with their normal wants, demands and flaws much of the shimmer is taken out of our silver screen. We feel let down because reality wasn't part of the original plot. Scott Peck claims that if at this point the relationship can't be turned into a deeper friendship, the long-term prognosis is poor. High divorce rates show that many a screen has tarnished over time.

The saying that we're 'falling in love' is also not without significance because we substitute the romance for ourselves. Although the other person is playing their movie, we try hard to live up to the starring role. Mostly we're a long way down the road before we even get onto what the Australians somewhat crudely call 'farting terms' – the time we allow our human nature to shine through. But good relationships are formed around common values, not fairy tales; and when reality kicks in romantic love breaks down. As it's rooted in an idealistic fantasy, it results in hurt and disappointment instead of the fulfilment we so desire.

The ideal prince and princess union is so deeply entrenched in our culture that we often confuse it with a close relationship. I have a friend who was madly in love (a good choice of words); and now after three years her partner claims that he loves her but isn't 'in love' with her. Translated, this puzzling sentiment means that I have a close affinity with you and we share many common good things; but what I want is lightning – all the time. Without constant electricity, he doesn't think that he can continue the relationship. Yet ironically it's the lightning of romance that destroys real love, often before it's even had a chance to begin.

ROMANTIC SEDUCTION

Many people are charmed by the madness of romance and, in pursuit of their fantasy, will often shift from one relationship to another. Sure no one wants to settle for an unhappy liaison, but few accept that compared to romantic love a close relationship is quite a mundane affair. It's about sharing your life in a comfortable safe space for both of you. It's not about going from one roller-coaster ride to another. Life itself stages enough surprises and if your relationship is a haven from chaos, it'll provide the deep satisfaction you desire.

I have a friend, Rita, who after nine years of marriage had an affair. She knew that it was wrong because it would deeply hurt her partner, John. But she was seduced by the thrill of romance. 'You know,' she'd say, 'I just can't talk to my husband the way Peter and I discuss things. It's not even about sex – which incidentally is great – but we just get along so well. We spend hours and hours talking and he's so much more loving than John has ever been.' Of course her lover was more arousing than John because she had no idea who he really was. During their few stolen moments neither needed to be themselves. They didn't have to put up with the uncapped toothpaste every day, nor did they have to deal with flaming moods or sulky moments. Any affair brings out the best in us, for a while. That's why they're so attractive in the beginning.

But for Rita the inevitable happened when John found out. She immediately put a stop to her illicit liaison and now they're managing to work things out. She and I were chatting over lunch and I could tell she was having a hard time because she really missed the excitement. Like her, many people have difficulty accepting that a good, close relationship is a routine concern and this is particularly true for those whose lives aren't exciting in themselves. These are usually the people most vulnerable when it comes to being attracted to a romantic affair.

TEACHING THE PIG

Our relationships are about sharing life; and if your existence holds little exhilaration, it's unlikely that your close relationships will be exciting. It's about what you bring to the party; and if your partnership is not satisfying you, it's not your spouse but your own reality that needs addressing. It's a hard fact of life, but it's true that we can't change anyone except ourselves. Trying to change your partner is a bit like teaching a pig to sing. It wastes your time and annoys the pig! If we keep irritating the pig, it's likely to be the harbinger for a short-lived relationship.

The easiest way to transform your relationship is to change how you respond to your partner. Mostly we have a small repertoire of responses. For example we may nag first and when this doesn't work lose our temper. If all else fails we then resort to a 'no-speaks' sulk and these three stages become a pattern in our relationship. But remember that in any area of your life, if you keep doing the same thing, you'll keep getting the same response.

So instead of nagging or having a cadenza, try something different. Use humour (not sarcasm!), be more accepting or put your foot down. But whichever, you're likely to get a different reaction. In the beginning don't, however, expect a favourable response. When you change the game your partner may get worse before he or she gets better. Brace yourself for this and be consistent with your new response. Eventually they'll come to accept it. Changing your response can also put an end to those countless discussions that go nowhere. If you've discussed the issue many times before but still nothing's changed, alter your behaviour and wait to see what happens.

DANCING CHEEK TO CHEEK

But you may have to dig deeper. Often these habitual patterns are a defence shielding us from a fear of intimacy. This fear of closeness is something I encounter frequently in the work I do. Now when I refer to 'intimacy' I'm not talking about sex because sex doesn't necessarily have to be an intimate act. Harriet Goldhor Lerner in her book *The Dance of Intimacy* defines an intimate relationship as 'one in which neither party silences, sacrifices, or betrays the self and each party expresses strength and vulnerability, weakness and competence in a balanced way'. Simply put, she says it's about being who you are in the relationship and allowing the other person to do the same.

So a fear of intimacy often starts with the fear of being oneself. If you don't accept who you are, the face that you show the world will be a social mask that covers for your low self-esteem. This impenetrable mask is what you bring to the relationship. Like a brick wall it prevents anyone from being let in. This includes partners, parents, friends and can even extend to your own children. It's frustrating because on the one hand closeness is so desirable and on the other so frightening.

BROKEN HEARTS

Social masks are created to protect you from the pain of having been hurt before. This may or may not have anything to do with being disappointed in love. It could also be from childhood. Trust is the glue binding any relationship; and many people have learnt that others can't be trusted with the depth of their soul. If you were hammered as a child for just being yourself, being who you are now is likely to make you feel intensely vulnerable. This is so because your bruised self-esteem is a constant reminder of this historic pain. But recall from an earlier chapter that emotional pain exists to prod you to learn something about yourself. No matter how old the pain is, if you're still feeling it, there's more for you to understand.

One of the residues left from broken trust is that we begin to lose trust in ourselves. We lose faith in our judgement, our ability to cope or even our own resourcefulness. Therefore if you're having a problem trusting others, retrieving your energy from old pain will help you to start valuing yourself. The lessons you may still need to learn are often to do with the fact that you're much stronger than you thought. That's why you survived those deeply painful episodes. Sure there will always be some people you're unlikely to trust again, but that's not the issue here. More important is that you learn to trust your feelings and yourself. When you do you'll have more leeway in your relationships.

Now if you're reading this thinking that your partner may fear intimacy, please read on. Being afraid of a close relationship is seldom something that only one person in a partnership experiences. If you've been thinking this then your best shot at intimacy is to look at yourself. In any relationship 'like-finds-like' and if your spouse is scared of closeness, he or she chose you for good reason. Subconsciously your partner picked up your fear and, for both of you, this was a guarantee against intimacy in the relationship.

This is what makes romantic love easy. Even with all those hours of talking and apparent compatibility, it seldom gets anywhere near true closeness. Of course it feels cosy when you're intimately living your own fantasy. But if both of you are on your best behaviour how can you really know the person sans the mask?

NEEDY AND CO-DEPENDENT

When fear of intimacy dominates a relationship it tends to move from romance to co-dependency. It's based on needing the other person rather than choosing to be with them. It's unfortunate, but this is the nature of traditional marriage. Still today, when people get hitched they're given the parlance that two become one in union.

Well, in all other areas of life two halves may make a whole, but marriage is definitely the exception. If two half people get together – hoping for the other to make them whole – they'll remain two halves experiencing large doses of frustration. Other people simply can't compensate for your emotional handicaps, so expecting them to will lead to much disenchantment.

Needing someone rather than choosing to be with them fosters high levels of insecurity. If your survival – financial or emotional – is based on someone else, you're no longer in control. This calls for great personal sacrifice, which makes it hard for either party to be themselves. Also no relationship can guarantee a deep sense of safety because others aren't always pre-dictable. These needs only create neuroses and jealousies, which place unnecessary stress on the relationship. Emotionally they just complicate our lives.

In your own relationship question how much of your togeth-erness is based on need or choice. You'll get a quick answer by asking yourself how much you like your partner. Like is differ-ent from love and if you answer 'not a lot', the reason you're together is mutual neediness. To resolve this, think how you could create more personal security for yourself.

This is important because your neediness is the greatest threat to the relationship. If you think about it, to meet your demands your partner has to compromise being himself or her-self. From the message of our emotions we know that this level of compromise makes us angry and angry people don't hang about for long. So your demands are like a wedge in the rela-tionship driving you further and further apart.

FULFILLED AND INTERDEPENDENT

Therefore, before we can truly love or be loved by another, we must learn to attend to our own needs. This is why chapters 3 through 9 are vital. They emphasise that the place to begin building good-quality relationships is inside ourselves. Instead of using our relationships as dumping grounds for our emotional baggage we must exercise more self-control. EQ also preaches self-reliance and this prevents us from confusing dependency with love. Only two relatively independent individuals make it possible to create a healthy interdependent union. Interdependence is a mature dependency – one that happens occasionally, not full-time. It's both reciprocal and appropriate and doesn't require either party to silence or sacrifice who they are. As such it allows the freedom to explore a truly intimate relationship.

Instead of seeing yourselves as one unit, interdependence suggests viewing your relationship as a ladder. The upright struts represent the two of you and the steps are the things that you have in common. Independence is depicted by the spaces in between, providing sufficient room for growth within the relationship. Co-dependent unions suffocate growth because to fulfil each other's demands both of you have to stay the same.

POWER GAMES

If your relationship is anything but interdependent, consider whether your need-to-be-needed created it. Many people suffer this affliction under the misguided belief that it makes them feel secure. But a need-to-be-needed has a lot more do to with power than security. In *Beyond Fear,* Dorothy Rowe describes power in relationships in terms of those who do the defining and those who accept the definitions. Dependents need you for their well-being so they appear to comply with the terms that you define. Here 'appear to' is the operative phrase because they never do this without a fight.

Although you are perceived to hold the power, it would be more realistic to state that your need-to-be-needed makes you vulnerable to their exploitations. But the battleground is seldom open confrontation. More likely, dependents will resort to all manner of manipulation. This is what's meant by emotional blackmail and it's used to swing the balance of power in the relationship. Based on Eric Berne's work *The Games People Play*, these manipulations can be divided into three categories: victim, persecutor and rescuer games. All three manipulations are control mechanisms. They're used by people, who aren't emotionally robust, to get their own way.

VICTIM GAMES

People who play the game of victim use 'poor me' to manipulate others. They are the ones who can't cope because they're always sick, hard-done-by or emotionally troubled. An essential element in the game is that their problems are caused by people other than themselves. Blame is a big victim game and you'll never hear them taking responsibility. Victims won't say, 'I got fired because I didn't perform.' More likely it will be the boss or the market, their spouse or family; but predictably someone else will be to blame.

When dealing with victims never be fooled by what you see. They act fragile, but they're powerful manipulators. They are stronger than both persecutors and rescuers because they control everyone around them.

I worked with a woman who had everyone in the palm of her hand. Her victim game was illness – usually the kind that's hard to diagnose. Benefit number one was the office speculation. It provided her with the attention she was seeking. As she was ill she could manipulate the bosses to work half day. Benefit number two – she got what she'd originally wanted. This also meant that financially she was struggling. But for a victim this meant that life was perfect. It gave her greater ammunition to do even more 'poor me' and you'd better believe she never let an opportunity pass her by. Now with all these problems, she had her sister and mother helping her clean her apartment and her brother did her weekly grocery shopping (benefits number three and four). But there's more. Often she was just too 'ill' to come into work in the morning and mostly this was disregarded – benefit number five.

If you look closely at the situation, it becomes apparent that this victim had too much going for her to want to change her behaviour. Why get well again when it meant having to take responsibility for herself? Clearly she had a vested interest in remaining sick and having everyone else run around for her. So yes, being the victim is powerful, but it means you have to stay miserable, sick or unhappy to remain in the game.

If you don't want to be on the receiving end of someone else's victim behaviour, make some rules for yourself. Victims are easy to detect because everything you say will be counteracted with 'Yes, but …'. Thereafter all the reasons why they can't change their situation will come tumbling out. Once you've recognised the game, become like a stuck record. Only respond by asking, 'So what are you going to do about it?' Soon they'll get bored with you and move on to others who will offer a more sympathetic ear.

Now for those of you who think that this may sound a little harsh, it's important to discern between a real victim of some unfortunate circumstance and those who play the game. Game players don't want your advice; they only want your ear. If they're not prepared to do anything to help themselves, I recommend that you run as fast as you can in the opposite direction. If you don't, you'll be left hearing different versions of the same story for as long as the relationship continues.

RESCUER GAMES

Rescuers are people who suffer from a low self-esteem and depend on helping others to boost their negative view of themselves. They're always there offering unsolicited advice and, unlike victims, rescuers take too much responsibility upon themselves. Rescuers are the classic 'need-to-be-needed' types.

They are controllers and use this to wield their power.

By their nature rescuers need problems to make sense of their own existence. As a result they will always be the one focusing on the difficulties in every situation. This is the fodder they thrive on. When faced with a problem they are quick to jump in and take over. After all, rescuers know what's best for other people! This makes them poor listeners and although they have a genuine need to help they often lack empathy.

Rescuers are usually in relationships with victims. They both thrive on the needs of one another and if you suspect that you may be a rescuer, take a look at your friends. If they're mostly needy victims, it would be safe to assume the rescuing label. You can be guaranteed that victims will find you because rescuers seldom have to go out and pick those who'll serve their helping need.

If you are a rescuer yourself, understand that you're not helping other people. People learn most from their own experiences and every time you jump in to solve their problems, you're robbing them of their own learning. It's unlikely that they'll ever learn to swim on their own if you constantly throw out a life-belt. Cure yourself of this game by understanding that rescuing does more harm than good and turn your energy to building your own self-esteem.

If you encounter rescuers offering unwelcome advice, tell them to butt out. Let them know that you're either capable of solving the problem yourself or will ask if you need their assistance. They may respond with a victim game, but their tears are easier to live with than their constant unwelcome interference.

PERSECUTOR GAMES

Persecutors are people who compensate for their poor self-image with a veneer of aggression. Often just the threat of hostility gets others to back off so they use anger liberally to gain control. If aggression doesn't get them their own way, they can turn nasty. Often humour is used – mostly sarcastic – as a foil. If you pull them up on it they'll say, 'But I was only joking!' and accuse you of having no sense of humour at all.

Persecutors play games that put other people down and they do this to elevate themselves. If you've worked hard on producing a report, they'll identify the slightest flaw and turn it into a big deal. Like the class bully they can also pick on the weak. They do this thinking they're endearing themselves to the stronger members in their class.

People who persecute are acutely aware of their own feelings of inferiority but will seldom, if ever, admit it. They also become incensed if others point it out to them. Usually they're the ones other people are afraid of. Because of this, persecutors usually experience a deeply felt sense of alienation. They are lonely and their need for control further distances them.

If you persecute other people, like the rescuer you'll need to work hard on your self-esteem. Remember from chapter 5 to learn to like who you are – warts and all. Your intolerance points to things that you don't like about yourself. So work on yourself rather than hammering other people. Greater self-acceptance is the only way to learn more tolerance for others. The healthier your self-esteem, the less you'll need to control others and this will increase your ability to form more satisfying relationships.

On the other hand if you are being persecuted, the best response is no response at all. Persecutors believe that everything that you say will be held against you and their memories tend to be long. Ignore their emotional hijackings and don't bother to react to their sarcasm. Always keep in mind that they're doing this to feel better about themselves. Once they're calm, point out their persecutor game and let them know that you won't be reacting to it in future.

Games are a product of need-based relationships and powerful players can fluctuate between all three games. They simply haul out the manipulation most likely to get them their own way. They can begin with rescuing to gain control and if this fails they may become aggressive. 'Look how hard I've tried to make you happy' is a favourite theme (when they've done very little) and if this too fails they're not beyond playing the victim. Manipulative games are a sign of a low level of EQ. They never lead to 'win-win' solutions.

THE 90/10 RULE

These games are destructive. They damage relationships; and people with a healthy level of EQ use more appropriate behaviours to get their own way. They know themselves, deal with their feelings and own their emotional baggage. To avoid the pitfalls of games, work with this rule of thumb: the problems you're experiencing are 90 per cent about you and only 10 per cent about the other person. Be responsible for your own actions and feelings and allow others to be 'response-able' for theirs.

The 90/10 rule also greatly eases communication. This is what I was referring to in an earlier chapter about communicating your feelings. First take ownership for the way you're feeling. Few people want to hear this but it's a reality that no one can make us feel anything at all.

Feelings are our response to a situation and we're free to choose how we react to every experience. Remember that your feelings are messages telling you to change the things you're struggling with inside of yourself. They aren't messages telling you to change other people.

Owning your emotions and dealing with them will relieve some of the anxiety and stress that you are feeling. Only once you've worked with the message is it wise to communicate with the other person.

INANE ARGUMENTS

When it comes to communication a further area to be addressed is our human 'need-to-be-right'. We all have a need-to-be-right, but it gets us into trouble when we inflict it on other people. This need is a facility we have to discern what's right for each of us in our own lives. It's like an internal guidance system that tells me whether my decisions are right for me and yours are right for you. And these will be different. However, if we're not using it solely for guidance it can get way out of control. Mostly it's activated by arguments. Arguments are a waste of time because no one's listening. They're too busy trying to make the other person see the error of their ways. It's a funny phenomenon, but when the mouth opens the ears tend to close and that's why nothing is gained by a need-to-be-right argument.

Prevent your discussions from turning into arguments by keeping your own need in check. If you don't, it's most likely either or both of you will end up having an emotional hijacking. Know when your need-to-be-right is coming through and take time out. It'll prevent you from fighting over something inane. Instead work towards understanding the real underlying issues. Aim to see things from the other person's point of view. Often both of you are right – you're just seeing things from a different perspective. Hearing someone else's point of view doesn't necessarily mean agreeing with them, but it will help you to learn and grow from their experiences.

BEING REAL

In all our interactions with others it's also important to know who we are dealing with. We're all different – we think and respond in unique ways, have learnt different lessons from our experiences and are driven by our own particular set of values. In other people, some of these you may approve of and others not. But this is not the issue. Just as it's important to accept who you are, life gets so much easier when we're also more accepting of others – especially those who are different from ourselves. These are probably the people who can teach us the most, but we have to get off our high horses to learn from them.

Self-righteousness is rooted in our need-to-be-right and it's a sign that we're stuck. Only by learning from our irritated reaction can we free ourselves from this self-imposed stagnant trap.

Knowing who you're dealing with also helps to avoid disappointment. For example, if you have a friend who embellishes stories, don't be surprised if he or she lies to you too. They're only confirming what you already know about them. Always look closely, and if they are devious in their dealings, why shouldn't they behave in a similar way with you? If you're entering a new partnership, friendship or close relationship, listen to how your new acquaintance talks about other people. It will reveal much about who they are and how you'll be treated in future.

FREE TO BE ME

Good close relationships are about immersing yourself in a deep friendship. Being with someone who knows you well and accepts and loves you for who you are is the most fulfilling human experience that we can have. Although close relationships may seem mundane, they're that much more rewarding because you can truly be yourself. Free from the many social façades demanded of you, your close relationships help you to find out who you really are.

To summarise, the characteristics of a mature close relationship include a high level of trust, the ability to offer mutual support and handle confrontation constructively, open communication, humour, fun, reciprocal growth, respect (especially around differences), warmth and the comfort of being with someone you like ... a lot.

Once a seminar delegate said to me, 'How come obituaries are always so flattering, but you never hear the living talk about each other that way?' It was a good question and the obvious answer is one that we can all learn from. Close relationships are the most precious gifts we have. Treasure them for we never know how long we've got.

Future forward

Last year I was contracted to a major insurance company to implement emotional intelligence training nationally. As always I began each seminar with a brief peek into the future. Here I mentioned that my research had led me to believe that within the next few years most people will be unemployed. I told them this not in the context of their company but in terms of what is happening all over the world. Mostly this tends to lead to a somewhat shocked reaction, but after a while you could almost see the defensive reaction kicking in. Many assumed 'that'll never happen to me' and training carried on as normal. Only a short year later this particular company merged and the accuracy of my prophecy began to dawn. Hundreds of people who had chosen not to hear these sentiments were taken by surprise when the reality of the retrenchment process started to sink in.

During this time it was interesting to assess who was coping and why. Those okay with the process were the most emotionally robust. They were not naïve about expecting retrenchments and had already weighed up their options. These hardy people were resourceful, knew their skills and felt confident that they would either find employment elsewhere or could start something on their own. Early into the process they were already making plans rather than waiting for things to happen. They looked at the process philosophically and many said it gave them a good opportunity to bail out of their comfort zone. Future possibilities and challenges excited rather than immobilised them. Interestingly, many of those with a healthy EQ were offered more challenging positions in the new company.

On the other hand, fear was rife among those who were taken by surprise. Many were out of control emotionally. These people had no idea of their next step and their insecurity brought out the worst in them. Not only were they disruptive, but they also lapped up and fuelled the negativity spread through the grapevine. Having entrusted their lives to the company, they were self-righteous and indignant about the way the business was treating them. Given their reaction to changing circumstances, these people were least likely to secure employment. After all, in an increasingly changing environment would you choose emotional retards to staff your business in this new millennium?

SECURE YOUR FUTURE

The point to consider here is that if you're currently employed, what are you doing to secure your own future? Don't assume like many of this company's employees that you're indispensable. No matter what unique skills you may have, it's likely that you could find yourself knocking on doors shortly. In most boardrooms around the globe discussions are being held about downsizing, outsourcing and the benefits of virtual offices. Even if your company is producing good results it's still no guarantee. To do better they'll have to get smaller. 'Lean and mean' has become today's business catchphrase; and it's not impossible that you just may be part of someone's slimming plan soon.

In chapter 1 we discussed that your only security in future will be what you can do or produce. Rely on it. If you're already self-employed this will have meaning for you. Many who've gone this route have found that they're much more talented than they gave themselves credit for originally. There's nothing like knowing that you only have yourself to bank on to push the boundaries of your creative spirit. So self-employment is nothing to fear for it can show you how capable you are.

However, if you still don't know what you can offer, make a list of your skills right now. Include talents that you've explored; and even if it's hard to see how you can make a living from them, write these talents down. Don't get hung up with what's possible or realistic because with a little imagination you can combine some of the strangest skills and talents into a most rewarding career.

An example of this is one of South Africa's most prominent motivational speakers. Starting his career as an accountant, Ian Thomas soon tired of bean counting. His first love was wildlife photography and especially the study of lions. He was particularly fascinated by the way lions harness individual strengths to maximise the chance of a kill. By combining this with his knowledge of business, he developed a profound analogy for management. Now he's making a great contribution strengthening leadership teams both locally and internationally.

Finding your own thing is not an easy task and it seldom falls into your lap. But if you explore more of yourself through new experiences, your unique contribution will reveal itself through your emotions. It will excite and inspire you and this is your cue. The strange thing too is that when you love what you do you seldom worry about money. Money is no more than a reward for contributing your energy; and when you fuel your career with love-based emotions, your high level of energy brings greater returns. One of the things successful people have in common is that they're happy doing what they do. So find what you like doing best and get someone to pay you handsomely for doing it.

TAKING BACK THE REINS

Another essential part of preparing for the future is taking back control of your life. This is what makes the future as forecast by authors like John Naisbitt, Charles Handy and Faith Popcorn so exciting. All point to opportunities for greater personal empowerment; and instead of having to bow down to the demands of others we have more personal freedom. Now you can become whoever you choose. You can discover your true potential and live it to the fullest extent. So make your choices, live them: and if you don't like what you've chosen, choose again.

Think about who you've elected to be and question whether you're robust enough for the future. Readiness for change requires having a healthy level of EQ. Emotionally it means knowing how to address your fears – particularly of the unknown – and being able to keep things in perspective. During challenging times having a clear vision in mind provides the necessary hope that will carry you through. Additionally, the ability to control your thinking and stop vomiting your complaints on others will keep you positively creating your life. All of these tools will conserve your energy – the fuel you'll need in abundance for the future.

DOING IT MY WAY

As you prepare yourself for the most stirring era in human times, remember that applying this material is a step-by-step process; and it's the process that's important, not getting it right first time. Every time you make a mistake or 'fail' you've gained some new learning in the process.

This is far more valuable than being perfect, which just keeps you stuck where you are. Keep questioning your responses and if you're unhappy with your own behaviour, change it. Apply the rule of the most appropriate behaviour for each circumstance and rely on your feelings to tell you if and when you're out of integrity.

Remember that EQ is not a model for doing the 'right thing' but rather for never again having to take 'no' for an answer. Applying your creativity to hatch win-win situations is the easiest way to get what you want. Cultivate your relationships, particularly those involved in your success process. Do what it takes to get other people on your side. Here I've had great results with something my mother taught me. 'Use a little charm!' she would say and this has been an invaluable tool to me in business – particularly with some of the more difficult customers.

Learning to get your own way will require change, but change is a subtle process. Human beings have an incredible capacity to adapt and change and you are no different. Accept that you're not fundamentally going to shift your old stuff overnight. Rather the trick is to work it a step at a time. In practice this is the one area that many people find difficult. But relax into the process and let it unfold. Your feelings will alert you to attitudes and behaviour that need modifying. Rely on them: they're an intelligent source of some powerful information.

Along with this unreasonable pressure for a 'quick-fix', another issue many people grapple with is that they think a healthy EQ means being positive all of the time. It doesn't. We're dealing with life, not making the movie *Pollyanna*. So no matter how high your level of EQ is, life won't be rosy all the time. Therefore to pretend that everything's good and fine – when it's not – is just white-washing your feelings. It won't help you to develop essential EQ tools for the future. EQ is about being real and if what you're feeling is anger – feel it – don't suppress it. Only by experiencing this emotion will the real message of your anger come through. This is information you can work with.

Often during my seminars delegates raise the fact that they're not unhappy about expressing their anger, but others are. Recall from the chapter detailing emotional hijackings that angry expressions are often destructive. If you're happy with this it's because you're being insensitive to the impact you're having on other people. Angry explosions will slowly erode your close relationships. Remember that whether you mean what you say or not, to some degree your venom will change their view of you forever.

GET IN TOUCH

A healthy level of EQ is about allowing yourself to experience all of your emotions. As in the above example, this is often confused with a licence to dump your baggage on other people. It's not. Rather it's about feeling the emotion to understand what it's telling you. It's a private personal experience, one where you're working towards making sense of your own feelings. Also when dealing with your emotions eliminate the words 'should' or 'shouldn't'. What are you going to learn if you keep telling yourself, 'I have no right to feel this way'? It doesn't matter what triggered the emotion: experiencing it is necessary for you to learn and grow into a stronger person in future.

Likewise, the most painful experiences will only reveal their lessons if you're in touch with your feelings. Many people deal with pain by denying it, largely to themselves. But this won't teach you anything. Denial only numbs you and if you want to be happy, at some stage you'll have to confront these issues. If you've been in denial for a long time, it's unlikely that you'll easily be able to identify what you're feeling. Don't label this numbness 'indifference'. This will only add another layer of denial, making it harder to break through eventually. Accept that you're currently out of touch with your emotions, but keep asking the question 'How do I feel about this experience?' If you don't get an answer initially keep asking the same question and in time the knowledge will come.

QUALIFY AS A MASTER OF EXPERIENCE

Remember that all experiences – especially the bad ones – have the potential to strengthen you, if you choose. And if you're going through difficult times currently, bear in mind that because of this experience you'll be much stronger in future. Sure life can be really tough, but trying events will only weaken you if you give in to them. Yes the process is often taxing, even exhausting: but if you fight to win through, concluding something to your satisfaction will energise you. A business I consulted to was proof of this. After a series of debilitating events – a number of which threatened closure – the team that emerged is now formidable. Prior to these incidents the business was loose, but to overcome the problems everyone pulled together. Only as a result of learning both individual and collective lessons have they now emerged as dominant market leaders. Indeed it's hard when tough times hit, but if you can focus on the fact that this experience will ultimately strengthen you, it's easier to pull through.

Learning from your experiences is the qualification you'll need most in the future; and the ability to apply this experience is now being prioritised over formal education. So much so that this type of person is being termed 'the knowledge' or 'gold-collar' worker and he or she is currently commanding the biggest income. Although some ten years ago the trend swung very much towards qualifications like MBAs, now the aptitude you'll need most is a high level of emotional intelligence.

My husband was amused by a conversation with a colleague who, in a large corporate company, had gone the route of acquiring this previously necessary qualification. He said, 'It's a strange thing, you know, that all those with MBAs stay stuck in middle management and just look who's running the show!' Apart from the financial director, the board members didn't have a post-graduate degree between them. It's a powerful endorsement of the potency of EQ. This sentiment was further reinforced by a discussion I had with some colleagues from Europe. Here being emotionally robust is the primary requirement for selecting senior people.

A high level of personal power will make you successful too. Although much of the personal growth literature has concentrated on developing the power of the mind, too many have focused on the ability to control our thinking. You'll recall from chapter 1 that our mental capacity is fuelled by emotional and spiritual energy and that's why controlling your thoughts is insufficient to make success a reality. The power of the mind comes from the spiritual, emotional and mental faculties. When you know what you want and can control both your thoughts and emotions you're a long way down the road to becoming emotionally intelligent.

REMOVING THE SHACKLES

Also I can't stress enough that developing a healthier level of EQ is a journey. It's a journey through life, one where you're constantly learning. There's never going to be a time when you can say, 'Well I've cracked it now, so I can stop growing.' This is what makes the journey so exhilarating. The first leg of this passage is always awareness; and the more conscious you are of why you make the choices you do, the more you'll learn and grow from your experiences. The awareness I'm referring to here is not a finite stage but more like a continuum. The more you develop this skill, the more acutely attentive you'll become to your own reactions. This will give you the necessary information to change behaviours that don't serve you.

Alongside the awareness stage comes a growing self-acceptance. Remember that self-esteem is the foundation of success and it's about accepting who you are. Included in this is acknowledging that it's your warts that make you unique and interesting. By simply getting through life, everyone has experienced trying times. We've all behaved in ways that we're not exactly proud of and have done things that have wittingly or unwittingly hurt other people. No one is alone in this. But how you've handled these experiences has built your character over time. It has made you uniquely you. Learn from this emotional baggage and it will lighten the load you're carrying.

A high level of personal power is the fuel of the future, so make sure you've retrieved energy trapped in past experiences. The interesting thing about aspects of yourself that you've tucked away in shame is that each one contains a character asset. Think about the traits that you've been lambasted for in the past and take a look at them again. I've always been accused of talking a lot and have been hammered for it starting at school. Yet if I didn't have this gift how would I conduct the seminars I do? A few people may not like who you are, but why let this dent your self-esteem? When it comes to our personalities understand that it's one area where you simply can't please all of the people all the time. It's part of accepting who you are.

Also in preparation for the future you, prioritise what's important and focus on it. We waste so much time on immaterial stuff and then don't get to the things that are really vital. Life passes quickly: ensure that each moment counts for something. Make the most of the things you do and know that you're already making a difference. You may not realise this now because we seldom have any idea of the impact our lives have on other people. Acknowledge yourself for the value you're creating by recognising that even something you say could change someone's life forever. In itself it's a great contribution.

IMAGINE ...

When it comes to making a contribution, many people feel that the golden period of new ideas is over – but it's just begun. We're already moving from the age of information into the era of imagination. This was encapsulated by Winston Churchill when he said, 'the empires of the future are the empires of the mind.' For us it means that many of the fortunes still to be made haven't even been thought of yet. Just look at the new industries that have mushroomed since Churchill's time. By projecting this accelerated growth into the future, we can get a clearer picture of the wealth of opportunities to be capitalised upon tomorrow.

We're moving into a far more creative time and to plug the imagination we'll need to learn to work differently. The imaginative spirit is not sparked by unhealthy stress levels and here it's no coincidence that leisure time has recently become more highly prized than long hours. Good quality relaxation provides a powerful platform for the imagination to run wild. I know good ideas just come to me when I take time out. To get new ideas going there's nothing like roaming the African bush or walking in the mountains. It's as if the imagination only starts working when our thoughts switch off.

The age of imagination will also draw heavily on our spiritual side. It's an age of enlightenment where we're getting more in touch with life's purpose and meaning. Now we can get beyond thinking that 'life's a bitch and then you die!' It's the era providing the ultimate freedom for the expression of our soul and it makes it an enormously exciting time to be alive. How you express your spirituality is an individual matter, but being consciously aware of it will determine whether you feel satisfied or frustrated in future.

THINK GLOBAL

Part of our spirituality is a greater commitment to taking more personal responsibility for world events. The age of information gave birth to the Internet, providing knowledge on any topic you may care to think of. It also offers a variety of opinions – expert and otherwise. Now there's no excuse to be uninformed about the shenanigans of politics, environmental damage and consumerism.

Knowledge is powerful and for the sake of our own well-being we need to respond with action. Too many decisions are made without fully thinking through the consequences and Y2K computer problems are just such an example.

Part of resolving problems in the ancient Native American culture was never to close an issue without examining the consequences for the children and their children's children. This issue was mainly considered by the older wise women. In this regard it's significant that the world is being 'feminised' and participative management is part of this trend. Feminisation is necessary to balance the previous emphasis on masculine forms of power and control. It brings in the Eastern concept of Yin. Now men are becoming more sensitised to these feminine principles which include creativity, teamwork, co-operation, sharing, compassion and peace. They are also important EQ values.

SCHOOLING NEW GENERATIONS

When it comes to consequences of a more personal nature something to consider is the way we're raising upcoming generations. Already their childhoods are a radical departure from our own and certainly their future will be unrecognisable. Here it's vital to give children the freedom to find out who they fundamentally are and coach their minds to become emotionally intelligent. Teaching them the skills of valuing who they are and learning from their own experiences will prevent EQ from declining further with each new generation. This is important for everyone because how new generations respond will influence all of our futures.

Also avoid denting their self-esteem because of shoddy grades or poor performance. In the bigger picture of their lives we know how unimportant these things are. Sure they'll need a certain level of education as an entry into business; but with self-employment on the increase your assistance will be more useful if you help them find their passion. Encourage them in what they're good at and assist them in accepting the areas where they don't excel.

Too often our imagination as adults is difficult to tap because it was squashed a long time ago. Encourage your children to explore their refreshingly innocent imaginations. It's something they'll need to rely on in future. Additionally, watch your own negativity. Whenever you're negative about the country, government or the state of the world, you're giving them the message that their future is hopeless. Rather teach them to be able to respond and remember that no child has ever been spoilt by too much positive reinforcement.

When parenting is boiled down, the most valuable gifts you can give your children are the security of feeling loved and a healthy self-esteem. Both will stand them in good stead when it comes to exploring themselves. These gifts will also prevent them from imposing their own will through an unhealthy rebellion. Get them to question everything – even if it's your behaviour – and this will help both you and your children learn and grow in a warm caring environment. Once they grow up, being in touch with who they are will give them the freedom to choose who they want to become. This is beyond your control. But you can give them a great start by allowing them the independence to explore and mature their own potential.

INTERDEPENDENT LIVING

Stephen Covey talks about maturity as moving from independence through to interdependence; and in Africa it's an ancient notion. In an earlier chapter I referred to this social concept as *ubuntu*. Although the media portrays Africa as a continent of violence, corruption, starvation and hardship, it has bred one of the most sophisticated and supportive social systems ever known.

While this has been grossly interfered with by colonisation, the system in its pure form is EQ in action. Instead of valuing money and power, *ubuntu* values people and community.

Practically it translates into living one's values and morality. It also involves a great deal of compassion which is underscored by a deep-rooted knowledge that no one survives nor succeeds alone. Events that impact upon the community aren't viewed as someone else's problem and, in one way or another, this means that everybody gets involved.

In our Western world interdependence makes issues like AIDS, world poverty, warfare and violence everyone's problems. As David Patient says about AIDS, 'It will either infect or affect all of us.' But what are we doing about these issues?

This new millennium brings a new era and each one of us can adopt an attitude of *ubuntu*. Practically it means just making our own contribution. This isn't difficult because by using our lives to make a difference we reap a host of personal benefits. Think about it. Can you imagine the extraordinary world we could create if everyone focused on adding value rather than trying to take whatever they can get? To do so we'll have to replace our scarcity-thinking with an abundance-mentality.

Without a doubt, this in itself will herald a golden era more powerful than any we've ever known. If we work on our own levels of emotional maturity and impart this to our children, it's possible. It only requires each of us being conscientious about the part we'll play in creating it. Mostly this means just managing our own lives: and for this we're all E-Qually responsible.

Appendix 1

Emotional dictionary

Use will-power to identify the feeling, understand the message and take action.

Emotion	Message or meaning	Appropriate action
Fear-based feelings and sensations		
Anger	Not getting your own way. Feeling forced to make a compromise that you're uncomfortable with. Anger warns you that the compromise may make you give up power. Anger is a wild general feeling often covering for hurt, fear or frustration. Identify what the real feeling is.	You need to analyse the compromise and decide whether or not you're prepared to make it. How will giving up your power in this instance affect you? Once you've made your decision accept it, live with it and let go of the energy. If it's covering for other feelings, work directly with these emotions.
Aggression	Acting out anger, which causes a tremendous loss of energy. It's a defence against feeling insecure or vulnerable.	Work with the message of anger. The loss of power has made you feel vulnerable. Work with this and you're more likely to get the tenderness you need.
Annoyance	You're tormented because things aren't going your way. Others won't let you take control and you need to be right. It's wasted energy and if left uncontrolled can snowball into anger and aggression.	Decide whether being right is more important than being happy! It blocks your ability to listen so use your will-power to control yourself because others may just have some valuable input to contribute.

Emotion	Message or meaning	Appropriate action
Anguish	Agonising over circumstances that could happen in future. It's a personal struggle because no outcome can ever be guaranteed. It wastes energy.	Do what you can do now and trust your own resourcefulness to manage the future as and when it happens.
Anxiety	Signals inner conflict – often between something you want to do and your fears. Power is being generated to accomplish whatever it is you're wanting, but fear of the unknown blocks your ability to act. This dams up energy in your system and yourbody starts responding (trembling etc.).	Look at the areas where you tell yourself 'I can't because of …'. Start by telling yourself that you can do it and slowly begin taking action – even in baby steps – to release the energy into your accomplishments. Accept that anything new will create anxiety – it's rooted in a fear of the unknown.
Boredom	Lack of growth and stimulation. Usually it's related to being in a comfort zone for too long. It slowly allows your energy to seep out of you.	Find a new challenge to stimulate your growth and this will stop the energy drain. Be committed to fulfilling your real purpose.
Depression	Loss of your life-force. Giving up. You've given your power away to the people who control you. Depression is a sensation driven by anger and resentment, but being unable to deal with these feelings you've turned them in on yourself. You'd rather compromise than confront others and this is how you've given them power over you. Depression blocks other feelings making you feel numb.	Firstly identify who these people are and why you allowed this to happen. Then go back in your history and analyse what needs to change in you. Start implementing these changes and with each small step you take you'll retrieve your power. The energy will make you feel better and relieve the depression. To avoid future depression keep focused on your soul purpose.
Disgust	Revulsion. Not wanting to be near or experience the object of your disgust. It's a message to move away from the person or situation before you lose power over your integrity.	Accept that there are some people and circumstances you may want nothing to do with. This is your right.
Distress	Extreme emotional pain caused by an emotional hijacking because of acute grief or intense fear. It's a chronic loss of power that separates you from your rational mind.	This is an emotion needing to be expressed. Stay with it until the tears are over and only then start looking at what you can learn from the experience.

Emotion	Message or meaning	Appropriate action
Dread	An extreme fear about the future. You're scared that a person or situation will cause a chronic loss of power that could immobilise you.	If the issue causing it is about your future, work with the action for fear. If it's a concern about your safety, take the necessary precautions and turn the dread into the opposite positive. Tell yourself 'I am safe' and this will help you retrieve power to reduce the fear.
Embarrass-ment	It occurs when you spontaneously make a blunder and it's a sign that your power is invested in how other people see you. Their views control your behaviour not your own needs. Maintaining the façade wastes energy, and if it slips you lose power quickly.	Begin by accepting who you are. Everyone is different so find out what's unique and special about you. Learn to like the attributes that make you stand out as an individual.
Envy	You are concerned that others may be or may become more powerful than you are. It wastes energy, making you more and more power-less.	Stop focusing on what others have got and start working on your own happiness. Learn to raise your own self-esteem and this will gene-rate more personal power for you.
Fear	Signals danger. This is only appropriate if your life is being threatened. Where this is not the case, it's a feeling coming from old negative learnt behaviour patterns. It's generated by memories of past experiences where you lost power. Fear consumes energy, and because of this loss you become immobilised. You don't have the energy to activate your inner resources like courage. It's debilitating.	If your fears are holding you back the only way to break through them is to do whatever it is that scares you. Start with the easiest things and work your way up to confronting bigger issues. Each experience will build your courage and provide new excitement. Soon you'll wonder why you were ever scared in the first place.
Frustration	Wanting something to change. Feeling stuck. If it's about your life, your feelings are letting you know you're risking boredom and stagnation. It happens when a comfort zone becomes uncomfortable. If it's about someone	Shift. It may be your attitude or circumstances that need to change.Whichever, find something stimulating to challenge you and the feeling will subside. If it's about someone else, accept you

189

Emotion	Message or meaning	Appropriate action
	else, you're wanting them to change their behaviour. Both waste energy.	can't change them so change your attitude to their behaviour.
Guilt	A fake emotion masking real feelings. It's wasted energy invested in 'I should, I ought to or I must do something' and it's a head-trip driven by other people's needs not your own. It's a learnt response to social norms (doing the right thing).	If you feel guilty ask yourself 'What am I really feeling?' Work with the message of the real feeling to make your decision or solve the problem. This will chase the guilty feelings away. If you shed the false image of yourself you'll feel less guilt over time.
Hate	Associated with fear of another person or situation. You have been hurt before by this person or someone similar and you're scared that they may have the power to hurt you again. You could also be projecting your own fears onto this person.	Soothe this feeling by assessing what these past experiences taught you about yourself and this healing will reinforce your own power. If it's a projection, start by accepting all sides of yourself – even the ones you've labelled bad.
Hurt	Emotional pain is energy trapped in an issue and it's telling you to learn something from the situation. This is usually about yourself. If it's old pain it means that you haven't yet learnt all the lessons from a past experience. Hurt occurs when there's an absence of loving energy.	Address how you care for yourself. Is your self-talk harsh and are you constantly lambasting yourself? If you are, this will make you prone to taking things personally. Be kinder to yourself and become more accepting of who you are and this will retrieve lost power.
Jealousy	Signals dependency. Concern that your own lack of power may not be enough to maintain the attraction of another person (spouse, friend etc.). This makes you fear that your relationship may end because other people have more to offer. It often is accompanied by hating the other person and anger.	Work on making yourself happy and you'll reduce the fear that's draining you. Move out of dependency by making some new decisions about yourself and act. If it's already reached the level of hate or anger work with the messages of these emotions.
Loneliness	Fear of intimacy. Inability to let your real self engage in your relationships. You're wasting power by maintaining	Work on finding your inner strength – you have more than you think. This will make it

Emotion	Message or meaning	Appropriate action
	the façade, and because you're projecting an unreal image of yourself are unable to get what you want out of your relationships.	easier to be vulnerable and let others know appropriately how to meet your real needs. It will improve your ability to truly connect to others.
Pride (false)	Fear of others' lack of respect. You are frightened of being humiliated. If you have built up an image of your own self-importance you are scared that it can come tumbling down.	What's needed is humility and an ability to laugh at yourself. Build up a strong self-image of who you really are – warts and all – and false pride will not dog your progress. Question how much you truly respect yourself.
Rejection	Occurs whenever you invest too much power in other people or your position. Losing either makes you lose that part of yourself.	Retrieve your energy by accepting that you have everything that you need inside of you to make your life great. You can be free if you start believing in yourself and your own abilities.
Resentment	The aftermath of anger. The feeling that you're left with after making a compromise you're unhappy with. It's the residue that calcifies within us and it turns into a bad habit. This is often why we're unable to forgive.	Stop blaming other people for decisions you've given in to. Forgive yourself first and start retrieving your energy by rectifying the unwilling compromises you've made. It's never too late to change them.
Sadness	Grieving for a loss. Loss – no matter what you've lost or given up – is always associated with sadness. Be aware of this when changing old habits. Change means we lose parts of ourselves and even if the change is for the better, the loss can cause a degree of sadness.	Grieve appropriately for the loss you've experienced. The bigger the loss the longer you'll need to grieve. If the loss is not significant wallowing in sadness causes such a loss of power that it will become depression. Ultimately it requires some kind of personal growth or transformation to heal the loss.
Shame	A deeper form of embarrassment linked to power invested in other people or social norms. It reminds you that you're human and have needs. It occurs when you judge	Accept that the perfection of human beings involves making mistakes; it's the only way that we learn. Instead of losing power over your gaffes, learn from them –

Emotion	Message or meaning	Appropriate action
	yourself to have behaved badly. If you want others to believe you're perfect, you'll suffer from a lot of shame.	even if they're in the past. This may involve learning to lighten up and laugh at yourself.
Stress	Pushing uphill. Either it's telling you that you aren't in control of the situation or that you are trying to cope using old habits rather than tapping into your inner resources. Like anxiety it's also excess energy without an outlet for release. Whenever you believe that you have no choice, you will feel stress.	You always have a choice, even if you're opting not to choose right now, and this leaves you open to being affected by other people's emotions. If you're pushing uphill against your old habits question why you do the things you do or even the way you do them. Channel the excess energy into creativity and find new, more appropriate ways of doing things. This will release the pent-up energy.
Surprise	Meeting the unexpected. It directs your energy to sharpening your senses.	Use the challenges to build your resources and this will contain your energy.
Worry	Worry hides your real fears and it's another head-trip masquerading as a feeling. It's like mentally rehearsing an imaginary event. It doesn't change anything for the better but only convinces you – through the power of repetition – that bad things are going to happen. Like guilt it's a total waste of energy.	When you hear yourself worrying rather use the power of your mind constructively. Stop yourself and turn the worry into the opposite positive affirmation. This will take will-power, but you'll feel much better when you cease imprinting negative beliefs.

Love-based feelings and sensations

Calm	A peaceful sensation that confirms your contentment with life. It's about feeling confident that you can generate enough power to master life's ups and downs.	Maintain the feeling; it will empower you to achieve what you want.
Courage	It's your undaunted spirit's ability to overcome fear. It's energy coming directly from the heart.	Keep this powerful energy flowing. The more you draw upon it the stronger you'll feel.

Emotion	Message or meaning	Appropriate action
Enjoyment	Acting on purpose. It's a great flow of self-sustaining creative energy.	Keep building upon it; it's the energy that moves you forward.
Enthusiasm	Love of life – every aspect of it. The stem of the word is 'en-theos' meaning inspired by God. The rush of energy that you feel is telling you that you're close to your purpose and gives you vital clues about your life-work.	Use the things you're most enthusiastic about to identify and keep living your life-purpose. It provides you with surges of natural energy
Excitement	A sensation of being ready or prepared for action. You're excited because you are in touch with your own potential. However, excitement can quickly turn into fear if you let your concerns or other people squash you.	Hang on to the excitement and channel it into creativity. It generates a massive amount of energy, and unless you direct it well, it'll quickly turn into fear. Stop listening to others' concerns. Rather believe in your own abilities.
Happiness	Feeling content with life. It's confirmation that your decisions are correct and that the path you're on is right for you. It lets you know that your system is well balanced and that your needs are being met (physically, mentally, emotionally and spiritually).	Maintain it by recognising any fear-based feelings that may come as warning lights. They'll let you know when your happiness is threatened. Stop, correct your behaviour with new decisions and take action. This will keep you happy most of the time.
Hope	A feeling that guards against despair. It's an inner confidence – a knowing that you can overcome the challenges you'll face in life.	Keep relying on your resourcefulness and you'll conserve your power through hope.
Joy	Satisfaction from acting on one's spiritual greatness. It's filled with happiness, enthusiasm and a love of life.	Go with the flow – it'll generate lots more energy.
Love	Wholeness: feeling fully connected to life, oneself and others.	Open up to lots more of this wonderful energy that feeds your soul.
Passion	Releasing positive power at full throttle. The more passionate you are the more energy you'll generate.	Channel your passion into successful pursuits. It's self-sustaining energy – the more you release, the

| Relief | The light sensation you feel once changes have been made and the pent-up power has been released. It tells you that you're retrieving your energy. | better you feel generating more of this great energy.

Use the energy constructively and it'll build into lasting happiness. |

Appendix 2

Self-esteem test

(From *The Psychologist's Book of Self-tests* by Louis Janda)

Mark each statement in the following way: if the statement describes how you usually feel, put a cross in the column 'Like me'. If the statement does not describe how you usually feel, put a cross in the column 'Unlike me'. There are no right or wrong answers. Read each statement quickly and answer immediately 'off the top of your head'. Do not deliberate at length over each one.

Like me   **Unlike me**

Like me	Unlike me		
○	○	1)	I spend a lot of time daydreaming.
○	○	2)	I'm pretty sure of myself.
○	○	3)	I often wish I were someone else.
○	○	4)	I'm easy to like.
○	○	5)	My family and I have a lot of fun together.
○	○	6)	I never worry about anything.
○	○	7)	I find it hard to talk in front of a group.
○	○	8)	I wish I were younger.
○	○	9)	There are lots of things about myself I would change if I could.
○	○	10)	I can make up my mind without too much trouble.

Like me Unlike me

Like me	Unlike me		
O	O	11)	I'm a lot of fun to be with.
O	O	12)	I get upset easily at home.
O	O	13)	I always do the right thing.
O	O	14)	I'm proud of my work
O	O	15)	Someone always has to tell me what to do.
O	O	16)	It takes me a long time to get used to anything new.
O	O	17)	I'm often sorry for the things I do.
O	O	18)	I'm popular with people my own age.
O	O	19)	My family usually considers my feelings.
O	O	20)	I'm never unhappy.
O	O	21)	I'm doing the best work that I can.
O	O	22)	I give in very easily.
O	O	23)	I can usually take care of myself.
O	O	24)	I'm pretty happy.
O	O	25)	I would rather associate with people younger than me.
O	O	26)	My family expects too much of me.
O	O	27)	I like everyone I know.
O	O	28)	I like to be called on when I am in a group.
O	O	29)	I understand myself.
O	O	30)	It's pretty tough to be me.
O	O	31)	Things are all mixed up in my life.
O	O	32)	People usually follow my ideas.
O	O	33)	No one pays much attention to me at home.
O	O	34)	I never get scolded.
O	O	35)	I'm not doing as well at work as I'd like to.
O	O	36)	I can make up my mind and stick to it.
O	O	37)	I really don't like being a man/woman.
O	O	38)	I have a low opinion of myself.

Like me   **Unlike me**

Like me	Unlike me		
○	○	39)	I don't like being with other people.
○	○	40)	There are many times when I'd like to leave home.
○	○	41)	I'm never shy.
○	○	42)	I often feel upset.
○	○	43)	I often feel ashamed of myself.
○	○	44)	I'm not as nice looking as most people.
○	○	45)	If I have something to say I usually say it.
○	○	46)	People pick on me very often.
○	○	47)	My family understands me.
○	○	48)	I always tell the truth.
○	○	49)	My employer makes me feel I'm not good enough.
○	○	50)	I don't care what happens to me.
○	○	51)	I'm a failure.
○	○	52)	I get upset easily when I am scolded.
○	○	53)	Most people are better liked than I am.
○	○	54)	I usually feel as if my family is punishing me.
○	○	55)	I always know what to say to people.
○	○	56)	I often get discouraged.
○	○	57)	Things usually don't bother me.
○	○	58)	I can't be depended upon.

RATING SCALE

To find your score, count the number of times your responses agree with the keyed response on page 198. The majority of the items do measure self-esteem, but the eight items on page 198 that fall under the heading 'The lie scale' are intended to identify people who were trying to present themselves in an unrealistically favourable light.

SCALE 1: SELF-ESTEEM INVENTORY

2.	Like	22.	Unlike	42.	Unlike
3.	Unlike	23.	Like	43.	Unlike
4.	Like	24.	Like	44.	Unlike
5.	Like	25.	Unlike	45.	Like
7.	Unlike	26.	Unlike	46.	Unlike
8.	Unlike	28.	Like	47.	Like
9.	Unlike	29.	Like	49.	Unlike
10.	Like	30.	Unlike	50.	Unlike
11.	Like	31.	Unlike	51.	Unlike
12.	Unlike	32.	Like	52.	Unlike
14.	Like	33.	Unlike	53.	Unlike
15.	Unlike	35.	Unlike	54.	Unlike
16.	Unlike	36.	Like	55.	Like
17.	Unlike	37.	Unlike	56.	Unlike
18.	Like	38.	Unlike	57.	Like
19.	Like	39.	Unlike	58.	Unlike
21.	Like	40.	Unlike		

SCALE 2: THE LIE SCALE

The following eight items comprise the lie scale. To find your score, count the number of times your responses agree with the keyed responses *below*. If your score was three or higher, you may have been trying too hard to appear to have a high self-esteem. You might want to take the test again with an eye toward being more honest with yourself.

1.	Like	20.	Like	41.	Like
6.	Like	27.	Like	48.	Like
13.	•Like	34.	Like		

Adult version of the Coopersmith Self-esteem Inventory:
Test-retest Reliability and Social Desirability

How do you compare?

Men	Women	Percentile	Range
33	32	15	Very low
36	35	30	Low
40	39	50	Average
44	43	70	Very good
47	46	85	High but caution

If you had an extremely high score on this scale, don't be too smug. There is some evidence that people with extremely high self-esteem may be that way as a result of defensive self-perceptions. We have all known people like this. These are the people who seem to exude self-confidence to the point of arrogance, but they show many of the signs of low self-esteem. They won't tolerate even a hint that they are less than perfect, they tend to be extremely critical of others, and they seem to have a need to prove to the rest of the world just how wonderful they are.

It seems to be the case that people with moderately high self-esteem are the most well-adjusted. Those with rigidly high self-esteem take themselves so seriously that they cannot tolerate any sign of potential weakness.

If you did score low on this scale, it does not mean that you are destined to a life of misery and self-doubt. First of all, keep in mind that this test was designed to be used with a normal population. It was not intended to detect mental illness. Second, many people gradually become easier on themselves as they grow older after they learn from experience that they aren't so bad after all. You can help this process along by making a conscious effort to pat yourself on the back for the things you do well. Remember, you don't have to come in first to be proud of your efforts.

Appendix 3

Growth review questionnaire

(Adapted from the book Why Smart People do Dumb Things by Feinberg & Tarrant)

This is a checklist to give you an idea of your progress. Tick each item to which you answer 'yes'. It doesn't matter how many ticks you have. What's important is to check your progress over time.

Complete it now and do so every six months to assess your progress. This will keep you focused on important aspects of your growth. It's like a personal appraisal; and when you see the progress you're making you'll be rewarded with more satisfaction in your life.

	In the past year	In your personal life	In your career
Have you gained more control over your emotions?	O	O	O
Have you gained more control over your thoughts?	O	O	O
Have you been on any personal growth workshops?	O	O	O
Do you have fewer emotional outbursts?	O	O	O
Have you been controlling your negativity?	O	O	O
Have you increased your reading?	O	O	O
Do you question more?	O	O	O
Do you have more fun?	O	O	O
Have your relationships become easier and do you enjoy them more?	O	O	O
Has your stress level decreased?	O	O	O

Growth review questionnaire

	In the past year	In your personal life	In your career
Have you increased your relaxation?	○	○	○
Have you made any new decisions about yourself?	○	○	○
Have you explored any new talents?	○	○	○
Do you believe things you never did before?	○	○	○
Have you turfed out some of your old beliefs?	○	○	○
Have you changed your routine?	○	○	○
Did you learn from your mistakes?	○	○	○
Do you find it easier to deal with other people?	○	○	○
Are you more focused in your activities?	○	○	○
Do you feel more motivated or energetic?	○	○	○
Did you learn any new skills?	○	○	○
Have you developed any new friendships?	○	○	○
Did you change some of your opinions about things?	○	○	○
Do you like yourself more?	○	○	○
Do you take pride in what you produce?	○	○	○
Have you become more inquisitive?	○	○	○
Have you become more flexible?	○	○	○
Do you review your beliefs about yourself, life, spiritual existence?	○	○	○
Have you become more sensitive to other people?	○	○	○
Are you more excited about life?	○	○	○
Did you achieve your goals?	○	○	○
Are you more committed to success?	○	○	○
Have you dealt with conflict appropriately?	○	○	○
Do you feel better about your life?	○	○	○
Have you given up any bad habits?	○	○	○
Have you developed any new good habits?	○	○	○
Have you stopped blaming other people?	○	○	○
Have you learnt anything from other people?	○	○	○
Has your health improved?	○	○	○
Are you any happier?	○	○	○
Are you more in control of your life?	○	○	○

Index